GameStop

How Reedit's Retail Day Traders Brought

(Secrets of Options Trading and Harness the Power of GameStop Phenomenon)

Stephen Castillo

Published By **Bengion Cosalas**

Stephen Castillo

GameStop: How Reedit's Retail Day Traders Brought (Secrets of Options Trading and Harness the Power of GameStop Phenomenon)

ISBN   978-0-9958936-6-5

No part of this guidebook shall be reproduced in any form without permission in writing from the publisher except in the case of brief quotations embodied in critical articles or reviews.

Legal & Disclaimer

The information contained in this book is not designed to replace or take the place of any form of medicine or professional medical advice. The information in this book has been provided for educational & entertainment purposes only.

The information contained in this book has been compiled from sources deemed reliable, and it is accurate to the best of the Author's knowledge; however, the Author cannot guarantee its accuracy and validity and cannot be held liable for any errors or omissions. Changes are periodically made to this book. You must consult your doctor or get professional medical advice before using any of the suggested remedies, techniques, or information in this book.

Table Of Contents

Chapter 1: Stock Market Basics

Supply and Demand

What factors determine the value of a share? It is easy to answer. The cost of stocks will be determined by the exact element that determines the value of everything else the market: demand and supply.

Every day when the market for stocks is open price of stock fluctuates as well as down, based on the quantity of sellers and buyers.

The amount of demand can be determined by the quantity of buyers interested in buying a particular stock at at a given price.

The supply level is based on the number of sellers who would be willing to buy a product at any time and at a given price.

If corporate stock is bought the buyers and sellers exchange cash to purchase fractional ownership. The latest price of a purchaser who has bought stock will be the price of that stock's latest value that can be viewed by the public market.

If demand rises and the price of shares in a company rises, it will tend to increase (just like every other product or commodity). This usually creates momentum for price towards an upward (or upward) direction.

When demand levels fall, a company's price of shares tends to go downwards, often and creates momentum that is in the bearish (or downward) direction.

This correlation essentially suggests that the stock market functions in the same manner as any other type of market functions in an ordinary capitalist system.

As supply rises the price decreases. If supply decreases the price rises.

But, it's important to remember that the availability of shares in corporate stocks is affected more than just the amount of sellers on the market, but also the amount of shares that are outstanding.

A company, for instance, might decide to offer new shares to the general public increasing the supply. In general, this can have a negative impact on prices.

If a business chooses to purchase back a portion of its own shares and sell it back, the amount of shares on the market is reduced and, consequently, reduce the total quantity of shares that are traded. This usually results in an impact on prices.

The majority of companies will buy back shares in instances when shares are cheap and they usually are made in the hope of pushing prices up to the near future.

The total value of a company is commonly known as the market capitalization (or "market cap").

Market Cap is calculated using the formula of multiplying the value of shares by the amount of shares in circulation.

As an example, a business that has a price per share of $50, and 10 million shares in circulation would achieve a market capitalization of 500 million.

The price of a $50 share x 10,000,000 shares outstanding equals $500,000,000 in market capitalization

Let's talk about options trading.

Options Trading

In the context of the GameStop incident, it's crucial to be aware of the options market along with the basic concepts of purchasing and selling stocks. So, let us move on.

Contrary to stocks, which offer purchasers ownership rights in the company that they purchase however, options grant investors the option (or choice, as the name implies) to purchase or sell an item (like the stock in this case) at a set cost on or prior to the date of a future date.

Each option contract the purchaser will choose an expiration date that is predetermined and a the price of stock that is utilized to decide the result of the option.

The date of expiration is commonly called"the "trade expiry" or "time to maturity" as well as the value of the shares is often called"the "strike price."

Today, the majority of call option contracts on the retail market are bought via online brokers and options are usually changed (or "rolled") later when adjustments have to be implemented.

When investors think the price of a stock will rise, "call" options are commonly utilized. When they do, the investors put their money on the fact that at or before the expiration date of the contract, the cost of the stock will to rise above the amount at which they'll be able to purchase it.

That is that they're purchasing the right to purchase at an affordable price or, in other words, a discount.

The profit is earned by the investor who decides to exercise his call option and buy the shares at a discounted price or discount before selling it on the market at more money.

It is vital to keep in mind this: investors aren't legally required to exercise their call options. When an investor makes a mistake and the price of a share falls below the strike price that the contract provides damages are only limited to the price originally that was paid for the option contract (also called"the "option premium").

So, the concept of options trading is distinct from stock trading as a traditional method. The potential for loss of the option market is limited and is clearly stated before the trade has been initiated.

In the end, it is clear that, while there's an element of danger that's typically associated with trading options However, it is essential to remember that risks are minimal and set in advance.

For example we will assume we want to purchase an option called a call that offers investors the chance to purchase 100 shares in Apple (NASDAQ: APL) at a strike cost of $125, with a duration which is 3 months into the future (which signifies the amount of time until the date of maturity).

The price (which is the value of the contract) can increase when the underlying value of Apple rises.

But, the price of trading could decrease in the event that the price of the stock falls.

When purchasing the contract, you can either hold on to the contract until the end of the term or even sell the contract if the market suggests that it is appropriate to exit. If we are able to hold this position through the date of expiration the position will be officially taken delivery of 100 shares AAPL for $125 for each share.

Naturally, the price for shares is available even when the market price of the shares is significantly greater. Let's suppose that rising trends of bullishness on APPL shares pushed share prices upwards to $165 in the three-month duration of our investment.

As the price of current shares is higher than what the price of strike is, each dividends on shares would be the same as the current price ($165) plus the strike price of the option contract ($125) as well as its price (which is dependent on the broker who trades it and the market's conditions). This is then multiplied by the number by 100 (since this was the quantity of shares initially defined by the option contract) for the final profits from the trade.

Okay. It's enough on calling options.

We'll now talk about options for putting.

As opposed the call option, which allow investors to purchase at a specific price, at a specific moment in the future"put" option "put" option is a trader's option that grants investors the ability to sell for a set price, at a specific moment in the future. The simplest way to describe it is that a put option is bought due to the belief that an investment is likely to fall to a price that's lower or equal to a certain price prior to some date in the near future (usually three months from now).).

Therefore that the worth of a put option contract increases when share prices are actually declining (or as interest rates fall). Put options, on the other hand, decrease in value if the prices of shares increase (or the time for maturity is near).

Similar to a call option the put option isn't necessary to exercise. Thus, the amount of money that could be lost through an option put contract is restricted to the value of the contract (also called the cost of contract).

Let us review. Call options are used to help investors believe that the price of a stock is heading upwards. Put options are used in cases where an investor is convinced that the price of a stock is downwards.

Call, up. Put, down.

In addition, we've realized that there are many kinds of trading instruments which can be utilized to make money in market conditions, bearish or bullish.

If an investor is convinced that an asset's price or market is declining, a different kind of deal that could be made is short selling. We will discuss the notion that short sales are a form of trading.

Short Selling

Adam Hayes who writes for Investopedia gives this definition of the traditional short-selling:

"Short selling" occurs when an investor takes out a loan on the security, then trades it to the public with the intention of buying it back at a later date with less.

Short sellers place bets on, and make money by a decline in a security's value. The opposite is those who invest long and want that the price rise." (Hayes 2021)

Based on this definition that short selling is extremely high risks. When an investor makes the short sale of the stock, but shares prices increase instead of falling when the trade is made then the investor is compelled to purchase shares back at a higher cost in order to repay (or settle) the money he or she the money was borrowed. Because there is no limitation to how much a stock's price could rise and down, the risk of losing is unlimited.

As we have discussed previously, the the risk of losing money of a put option is restricted to the sum the initial payment is made by the buyer to initiate the option.

So, even though the short and put option are bearish varieties of trading, the levels of risk associated with them are significantly distinct.

As an example, let's imagine that we buy an option for three months in MSFT stock with an exercise cost of $235 for each share. If this is the case the stock must observe the stock's decline in value before we can achieve profitability within the trade. If instead, the stock makes an unanticipated move in the bull market for example, $285 per share, following the release of a positive report on earnings within this period then we won't use the put option (or option to sell) which means that the amount that we'd lose is similar to the amount we spent to buy the option (which typically is not much, when viewed in terms of relative).

But, had we taken a short-term option instead of buying an option called a put and we were liable to losses of around $5k on an exchange of 100 shares. If we consider this scenario, it's not hard to understand why a modest premium on an contract is much less than the costs that be incurred if we opt for a straight short position.

The understanding of the significant risks associated with short selling is crucial in the context of the GameStop account.

Additionally, it is extremely high risk, it's also crucial to remember that selling a stock short at a high rate (volume which can typically be attained only by institutional investors) increases the cost of the stock. Due to this, it's easy to understand the reasons why this method of trading is also viewed as controversial and as extremely risky.

Then Elon Musk famously stated on January 28 2021 "u can't sell houses u don't own, u can't sell cars u don't own, but u *can* sell stock u don't own!? this is bs - shorting is a scam legal only for vestigial reasons"

What exactly is an'short squeeze?

Naturally it is true that the GameStop tale is comprised of lots of jargon, technical and market language that could be confusing for readers who have no exposure to investing. However, now that we know the fact that investors are able to profit from both negative and positive economic trends, it's important to know how the strategies may be a disaster. It is necessary to provide an explanation of a further piece of terminology used in investment that is crucial in analyzing the rise in prices for shares that will end up being seen on shares of GameStop stock in the Jan. 2021 period of trading.

There are a lot of distinctive aspects in this tale that have been virtually incomparable within the past history of market, the idea that is"short squeeze "short-squeeze" has been one of the most talked about phrases in media coverage. Short-squeeze is a regular occurrence that's been used in the context of short-selling in its own. Though the vast majority of people on the market focussed on buying and holding strategies (which profit when shares prices increase in value), Wall Street hedge funds can access many different creative strategies that are able to make bets on price changes across any direction.

We have discussed this before that short selling is a way for the investor to obtain shares of their stock to determine whether the value of their shares is likely to fall over time. If those expectations prove to be true, bearish investors are able to buy back these shares (at lower prices) and make money from the difference. If, however, those hopes prove to be wrong (and the prices of shares rise after the short-term trade has been initiated) these bearish investors must buy back the shares at higher rates. As investors are required to pay an additional amount for the difference between beginning and closing price which results in losing the position. Furthermore, short-term positions usually are subject to expiration dates and when prices for shares rise in a sudden manner short sellers often are called upon to respond quickly in order in order to reduce the losses.

In the event of sudden price increases in shares, it typically amount to the "worst case scenario" for those who trade on the short end of the marketplace. This can lead to the exodus of all investors seeking to sell their short-sell position. In essence, this causes an influx of open positions on the market as bearish investors buy back shares after the short-term trades close. If these developments are large enough to trigger a massive growth in purchasing activity that results in an "short-squeeze" that sends share price up.

According to the old saying, an unexpected purchase "squeezes" the market's short sellers of their positions, and a lot of the bearish investors will likely face loss in trading. Examples of this kind of behavior were observed in the case of shares from Tesla, Inc. (NASDAQ: TSLA) attracted a substantial amount of interest from shorts during the early part of 2020. The those who were bearish saw the company as an overvalued asset, and placed bets on the market's increasing interest in Tesla's yet-to-be-proved ability to outperform conventional automakers, and also to market electric vehicles to consumers of all ages.

In this time, TSLA became the most frequently shorted stock within the United States (with nearly 20 percent of Tesla's outstanding stock that investors had sold to short). But, the steady rise in the price of shares gradually caused investors who were bearish to leave their stakes and this brought gains of about 400% in comparison to the market value towards the end of the year. The end result was in staggering losses in the region of $40 billion for the short-selling industry while shares of TSLA continued to post an annual gain of 743 percent for the entire year for 2020.

We can observe that the short squeeze may occur due to some bearish investors take positions based on the notion that the value of a stock is likely to decline over time. But, those expectations could be shattered when a good financial performance or a favorable information story alters the prospects and triggers an increased quantity of traders to create large positions in the company. In certain instances an upward trend in prices of shares could be temporary. However, if the upcoming prices are bullish enough, they could cause short sellers to seek off their cover and sell their shares to protect themselves from more loss.

For protection to protect yourself, the most effective method to know if a particular share is most likely to suffer an immediate short squeeze later on will be to examine the short interest rate (which is the ratio of shares that are sold short in relation to the total number of shares in circulation).

Another method that is more complex is to look at the ratio of short interest in the stock (which divides the amount of shares short sold by the daily average volume of trading). Both ways the higher number suggests a higher risk of the possibility of a short squeeze on the shares. The same analysis can be utilized as a method for determining the likelihood of high volatility of any equity market asset.

In our analysis of the historical GameStop short squeeze, stocks that are speculative that are small-cap sized typically have higher rates of short interest contrasted with larger corporations. However, the relative change of a company's short-interest amounts can be seen as an important indicator to determine if the market's opinion is shifting about the prospects for the company in question.

A stock, for instance, that is typically subject to the short interest range of 20% to 40% may experience dramatic variations in the price of shares in the event that short interest goes over (or decreases to below) the historic interval.

The rise in short-term interest typically suggests a higher degree of optimism on the market (which may lower the value of shares). However, if they reach extreme levels, stocks is more vulnerable to the risk of short-term squeeze (which could result in an explosive rise in the price of shares).

However, the decrease in short-term interest suggests a greater sense of optimism the market (which usually sends share prices up) which decreases the likelihood that the stock could be hit with an unexpected short squeeze to come in the coming years.

What is Market Manipulation?

Market manipulation is a crime within the United States and is defined in the US Securities Exchange Act as "transactions which create an artificial price or maintain an artificial price for a tradable security" (Wikipedia, n.d.). That is the act of an investor in order to manipulate the value of an investment with intent of gaining profit by the fluctuation in price can be regarded as manipulating the market. The majority of times it is very difficult to carry out given the magnitude of the business targeted is in "large-cap" status (In general, "large-cap" refers to firms with a market value over $10 billion (11)). But, "small-cap" or "micro-cap" stocks, such as GameStop for instance, may be a target to market manipulation that is illegal because they typically do not fall within the scope of the analysts and are not often reported by news outlets covering financial matters.

In light of that, a lot of experts questioned whether excessive short-term strategies that some Wall Street hedge funds against small-cap stocks that were struggling did not violate lawful "spirit of the law" because these strategies may create artificially low shares prices.

Chapter 2: The Reddit Rebellion

We now get to the part of the tale which are revolutionary by nature. When we consider the history over the years of financial markets, the majority of the top players employing short strategies were individuals working in hedge funds that were located on Wall Street. Although anyone could be technically competent to sell an equity, the truth is that a lot of smaller investors may not understand the meaning of "short-selling" is. Additionally, the smaller players in the market are not able to access the money needed to build an adequate defense against more powerful investment entities which frequently engage in short selling stocks.

In the GameStop report the online forum of traders with a contrarian outlook looked at companies that had significant levels of short interest in Wall Street's hedge funds. In order to take advantage of the increasing likelihood of the investment industry to become a victim of a huge, short squeeze trading forum on Reddit known as WallStreetBets (r/WallStreetBets) looked at GameStop's short-interest rates and found that the stock's heavy, single-sided positions for the stock revealed serious vulnerabilities for institutions.

It is evident that two parties were the main players at the time of these incidents. One side were dealing with the institution which is represented by hedge funds operating in Wall Street. On the other hand there's a gang of individuals trading on the social media site Reddit as well as adopting strategies that are contrarian to the stock market that are largely ignored in the eyes of investors. It's surprising that this group was able to exercise an enormous amount of influence that was entirely surprising and caught many members of the financial analyst community out of their element.

In the course of time, financial media began using the term "retail traders" to describe these private investors who operate outside of the boundaries of Wall Street as "retail traders." In essence, this word is a bit of a joke and refers to traders who are not professional and take positions through brokers online as well as other kinds of second-party investment accounts. Because these investors aren't thought of as having "direct access" to the market (and frequently invest with accounts that are small by value) and are generally thought of as less important as regards the effect their position could have on market prices.In contrary, the phrase "institutional investors" refers to organizations (usually professional hedge funds or portfolio managers) who initiate investments of a large scale and typically operate from upscale regions (such like Lower Manhattan, Tokyo, or London) in order to have more access to clients with wealth. Given that the vast size of position that institutional investors take on tend to aggregate huge amounts of money and thus the effect that institutional investments could have on markets is usually regarded as significant.

In order to combat the disadvantages mentioned above, to combat some of these disadvantages, the Securities and Exchange Commission (SEC) established goals to safeguard investors in retail from fraudulent brokerage practices as well as to guarantee orderly operations on the financial markets. This is why the SEC gives educational material to consumers and provides resources which enforce rules to boost trust while making sure individuals feel confident trading in financial markets. (White, n.d.)

As we'll read in the pages to follow which will detail the events that led to the GameStop incident, this class of investors who are small scale isn't at all as slender and vulnerable as they might have been before.

The development of the internet in the last 20 years has brought about a level competition in the field of short selling in various ways, principally through decentralizing information and knowledge and also by offering a variety of broker platforms that any could make use of.

However, Reddit Rebellion Reddit Rebellion demonstrated another way that the web can assist in bringing the level playing field to a more equal one with social media. Incredibly, the community of known as "retail" investors has proven that they are able to affect financial markets in significant ways.

The number of active trading communities social media platforms are present for a long time, and in ever-growing amounts, the potential of these communities to collectively be competitive with institutions has not been recognized until recently. Tim Collins who writes for RealMoney.com declared:

"There's become a resurgence. An entire group of retailers have discovered that the power of working together making use of market instruments such as calls that are out of the money or stocks with a low floating, they could outsmart any bank or short-selling business in the world. This is not including the Fed Of course." (Collins 2021)

The more affluent segments of the investment world are able to access trading strategies that take advantage of markets that are prone to downside and combine them with the potential that social networks offer, it is be sure that Wall Street's dominance of short-selling will decrease over time.

These new trends are just beginning to take shape and the latest developments within the GameStop stocks have exposed the unidirectional nature of these methods as they're being implemented across the world market.

As of January 20, 2021, around 140% of the GameStop's "public float" (which is an expression that means the quantity of shares in the market currently) were short-sold. If you're a new investor It may seem unimaginable (or perhaps it's difficult to think) that more than amount of shares that are available to the public market could be short-sold at any point in period. This scenario, however, is not atypical, suggesting the strength to be a part of Wall Street is sometimes incomprehensible and these kinds of scenarios are susceptible to disruption for some time.

A brief explanation here of the book's title. There is a chance that you could be thinking "What does stonked mean?" The general meaning of the English phrase "stonk" is typically used as a word used in military slang that means to assault with artillery gunfire. However, like all slang it is employed in various ways, and none have anything at all to its military origins. In some instances, for instance, it is used as a reference to someone who's really drunk. Or drunk. Or both.

Chapter 3: The Timeline of Events

August 2020

Over the years, GameStop had been a brick-and-mortar institution; a symbol in the gaming world. It was, and remains, a location for gamers to purchase or trade games on video. But the advent of digital technology of gaming has made it simpler and quicker to access video games instantly by downloading them onto a gaming console. This innovative method of buying was a threat to GameStop's brick-and mortar model of business. It was widely believed that it would only be the beginning of the end before the brick-and-mortar king would be an era of its own. In the world of institutional investment the jokes of GameStop being the next Blockbuster film were becoming commonplace.

As per Wedbush Analyst Michael Pachter, GameStop's physical disc-based gaming business was in serious trouble, and it was only a an issue of time until the company would be facing complete collapse.

"I definitely think it's a melting ice cube. For sure it is going to go away eventually. And for sure their future will be truncated and eliminated the day that discs stop being manufactured." (Gilbert, 2019)

Unfortunately, the inability to keep up with changing market conditions saw the footfall of GameStop drop by 3 percent in 2019. The year following (in partly due to COVID-19 lockdowns) GameStop experienced a dramatic 27.3 percent drop in foot numbers.

In August, 2020, Ryan Cohen, co-founder of the online retailer of pet products Chewy, Inc. (NYSE: CHWY), disclosed the details of a 5.8 million share part in GameStop Corp. (NYSE: GME) through a file to the Securities and Exchange

Commission (SEC) and caught the attention of the financial market off guard. This stake was worth 9 percent of the total market capitalization. However, Cohen's investment group didn't stop from there. In order to further expand its market share GameStop, RC Ventures continued purchasing GME stocks in the months following. In December of 2020 it owned more than 13 percent of the video game retailer's shares in circulation.

During the time of intense acquisition, Cohen publicly made the assertion that GameStop ought to shift away from its earlier reliance on brick and mortar stores' sales and instead focus on games on mobile, online, and online sales. The complete correspondence Cohen addressed the GameStop Board of Directors can be downloaded here.

Based on Cohen's his success in the world of e-commerce and his track record of success, it's no surprise that this bet with high stakes on GameStop was noticed by merchants from around the globe.

Afterall the shares of Chewy Cohen's highly profitable e-commerce business, been up more than 350 percent in the prior 13 months (from November 2019 until the end of December in 2020). Such huge returns could make anybody who is looking to make a difference, and think of following in Cohen's footsteps. That's exactly what they did.

A discussion thread on Reddit that is referred to by the name of the subreddit WallStreetBets that's made up of retail traders who are independent and investors, jumped into the conversation and continued it. In the case of many group participants, Cohen's announcement drew their attention to a brand new purchasing possibility.

After it was revealed by public records the GME stock was heavily shorted by investment companies of institutional size (for the reasons clear for the members of the group) The gears began to be set into motion, which was able to accelerate Wall Street and Main Street toward a massive confrontation.

The months prior to the release in December of GameStop's quarterly profit report GME stock price GME stock increased by nearly 230%..

Dec. 8th, 2020:

The ebullient momentum of GME stock slowed for a brief slowdown when the company published its earnings report for the quarter on the 8th of December, 2020. The report showed a significant decline in revenues for the company, mainly because of the closures of stores in the COVID-19 lockdown. Furthermore, these results from a backwards perspective caused the possibility that GameStop had fallen further behind with regard to its capacity to adjust and benefit from recent trends in the digitization of gaming online.

The following day the shares of GME fell to sessions lows of $13.23 that was the decline of almost 32% from its highest levels of the month before.

In the perspective of investing the event is significant. Members of the online group that are part who are part of the WallStreetBets trading community saw this as a great opportunity to buy. The correction in price was not long-lasting and GME shares continued to climb on a ascending trend.

Jan 11th, 2021:

On the 11th January 2021, the board of GameStop appointed Ryan Cohen and two more veteran e-commerce veterans into its roster. This strategic action sent an unambiguous signal to investors that GameStop is serious about its new digital strategy. Yet, when these announced strategic changes were being made, the short interest for the stock stood at 7 million shares. This was sufficient to limit GME price with a price of about $20. This cap on price suggested that the institutional investors of Wall Street were failing to pay attention to GME's new outlook.

It was obvious that GME was one of the stocks that was most hated by the Wall Street investment community.

On Main Street, retail traders in the Reddit trading community saw these low price estimations as a chance to purchase the long GME stock in spite of the terrifying resistance they'd face by Wall Street short sellers.

The immediate effect of these trading moves within the Reddit community led to an increase in GME shares. In the trading window of just one session which followed GameStop's announcement that it would nominate Ryan Cohen to its board, GME stock gained by 12percent.

The battle between the two selling and buying forces began to heat up. Markets were in the moment of an historical short squeeze that would send GME stock to surpass $480.

Jan 13th, 2021:

In January of 2021, the gloves went completely off, and purchases within the Reddit group resulted in GME share prices up by 57% over the course of one session. For the context of bullish trading, this action helped GME shares to move through a trading range which lasted for nearly two decades and, in the end, these gains led to the most significant single session rally in GME's past.

In a departure from the traditional pattern of selling low to buy high The Reddit group continued to purchase while share prices shot up. This action pushed the share price up to a record maximum of $39.90 within the subsequent trading session (a movement that showed the single day gains of 27 percent).

In another way, to illustrate the power of what was at the time called Reddit Rebellion, another indication of the strength Reddit Rebellion, it should be pointed out that, at the time of writing, the price of GME shares had exceeded its average analyst price goal at $12.50 per share. This was by almost 220 percent.

Many investors felt that these events ruined many of the longest-standing ideas in the field of finance. Wall Street's credibility opinions on what the proper worth of equity-related securities was transformed into something that was almost insignificant.

Another thing that is surprising is that the scale of these changes was not completely realized. In many ways, the first rallies in GME price helped draw more focus from the main financial news media. The media's attention is the primary factor in putting the stock that was once a secluded one in the spotlight for confident investors who were eager to push GameStop far, far higher.

Jan 19th, 2021:

After the media covering the financial sector had joined the bandwagon and following the storyline of this historical event The Battle Royale being waged between the hedge funds on Wall Street (the selling short) and the Reddit's traders at retail (the buyer who is bullish) appeared to be growing in force.

The 19th of January, short-sellers from Citron Research fired a Twitter assault on the Reddit group, calling into question the capability of the community of retail traders to compete with big banks that been the dominant force in the financial market from the beginning. The tweet stated:

"GameStop GME customers... They are being sucked out of this game. The stock is back up to $20 quickly. We know more about short-term interest than you do."

For many, the publicly displayed display of smugness targeted at the trading industry's retail traders appeared to signal the arrogance of Wall Street's Wall Street institutional investment class overall. It is now clear that the tweet served as the catalyst that the flame needed to ignite.

To give you a to reference, GME shares traded in the range of $34-$45 per share during the time Citron's flamboyant attack was launched at Reddit. Reddit trading forum.

Unfortunately, for Citron Research, the firm was in the wrong place of the betting. Seven trading days later the infamous short squeeze triggered by the WallStreetBets trading group on the internet would oblige GME shares to trade for 10 times more ($483 for each share) than at the time Citron posted its tweets attacking the community of traders who retail.

A few days later and in what could be described as a genuine retribution Citron Research founder Andrew Left made a video of an apology public announcement. The apology was in reaction to the on-brand tweet which he had posted within 10 days of the tweet. The following is an excerpt of the entire video which can be viewed below:

"20 year ago," I founded Citron to be a means to protect the person against Wall Street, against the fraudulent stock offerings and frauds which were then gone. When we first started, Citron was meant to be a counter-weight against the establishment, but we've turned into the establishment. As of today, Citron Research will no ever again publish what might be termed short-selling research reports."

The public apology and the rising cost of GME stock, almost entirely out of displeasure with the powerful wigs in Wall Street, showed that the Reddit trading community's capacity to take on all the giants of Wall Street had reached a degree of power which was unquestionably evident. A new market force had arrived: trading populism.

Jan 22nd, 2021:

GME shares GME recorded an additional 51% single session gains on the 22nd of January. It was evident the fact that Wall Street was becoming concerned over the repercussions of the stock's short squeeze and trading in GME shares was stopped through the SEC (on multiple occasions) in response to the SEC's description of "excessive volatility."

In accordance with the U.S. Financial Industry Regulatory Authority (FINRA) it is the SEC has the authority "to suspend trading in any stock for a period of up to 10 business days... when it believes that the investing public may be at risk." Most of the time the situation arises in the event that a business fails to keep proper records of its quarterly or annual earnings reports that are designed to give the correct details (such as financial performance or the company's outlook by management) which is required by investors in order to make informed trade decisions. A further reason that the SEC may suspend trading on the stock could be in the event that the accuracy of information provided by a company's publicly available sources could be suspect of being inaccurate.

In the end, when trading in GME shares was stopped by the SEC the decision was not due to the above reasons. The SEC's decision to stop trading on GameStop shares was due to GME's unusually volatile trading and it is possible that market manipulation caused the prices of shares up. As no evidence for manipulative market activity was discovered the shares of GME traded on the marketplace and hit a record-breaking high on January 22.

Jan 25th, 2021:

The momentum-buying trend continues to push the price of shares up, GameStop stock added gains that could reach 144% over the course of a single trading day on January 25th. In the midst of ongoing debate regarding the possibility of excessive markets and fluctuations the trading public of GME shares was again stopped in nine instances.

In CNBC, Jim Cramer said, "The mechanics of the market are going through a break. ... The market has not seen guns as powerful as these. They are able to cut shorts."

In the case of many traders who trade retail, attempts made of the SEC to stop buying within GME stocks violated the basic principles of fairness in capitalist systems.

Jan 26th, 2021:

The 26th of January, 2021 Elon Musk shared his famous tweet "Gamestonk!!" It also contained a hyperlink to the WallStreetBets discussion forum on Reddit. Responding to the affirmative tweet WallStreetBets users rewarded Tesla's Tesla chief executive with a fresh nickname: "Papa Musk."

It is the norm whenever Elon Musk gives his seal of approval for some thing, his tweet had a positive effect on the share price and GME finished the session in the 92% range over the trading session. While the market tensions continued to rise and trade activity slowed, GME shares was stopped at five different times on January 26th.

William Galvin, the Secretary of the Commonwealth of Massachusetts, said in a written statement addressed to Barron's, "This is certainly something I'm keeping an eye on. It concerns me because it indicates that there's something fundamentally wrong with the options that are traded in this particular stock." (Salzman 2021)

Jan 27th, 2021:

The 27th of January saw the short sellers Citron Research and Melvin Capital have allegedly resigned their bearish positions on GME. The shares hit levels of $380 in the day, short squeeze actions by the r/WallStreetBets r/Wall resulted in substantial losses for institutions hedge funds and traders that were taking massive short positions in the stock. Furthermore, once short-squeeze trades have been closed, they change into longer, new trades (to pay off and settle the positions).

In the end, large institutional investors were basically putting buy orders on the market as they shut down the GME position in short. This activity ultimately led to the price of stocks going up to levels which only a handful of analysts could have imagined possible.

In the meantime the amount of users of the subreddit r/WallStreetBets increased up to 5.2 million. In order to catch up with the torrent of posts that were posted, the moderators of r/WallStreetBets were forced to shut down the site during trading hours. The forum was eventually locked to be it was an "invite-only" page to manage the increasing number of new members.

Jan 28th, 2021. The 28th of January, 2021: Robinhood trading platform provoked anger among its users in the form of limiting further purchase of GME stock, but permitting the selling of the shares.

In addition, the platform for trading stated that the margin requirement would be increased when shares are purchased from GameStop this meant traders need to contribute more capital in order to fund bigger trades.

Robinhood's website's message was:

"We constantly monitor markets, and implement changes when required. Given the the recent volatility, we're making certain that transactions on specific securities are restricted for closing of positions to only."

The news sparked anger among many in the community of retail traders as well as outside. The most skeptical thing regarding this change was that Robinhood has stopped traders from purchasing GME shares, however they were not prevented from selling the shares.

Some critics claimed that this unilateral policy, though only temporary, gave an unfair advantage to hedge fund and institutional investors who held short positions in the stock. The stopping of buying the stock could temporarily halt prices from moving upwards, while still allowing the sale of the stock could in theory push prices lower. Both scenarios would be beneficial to short-sellers in the institutional market by stopping more loss.

It's important to remember the fact that Robinhood is not a brand recent trading platform that was founded in 2013 and whose stated goal to "provide everyone with access to the financial markets, not just the wealthy". Robinhood aimed to achieve its goal through removing fees and providing an intuitive interface that can be easily understood by novice investors. In light of its mission the trading platform been gaining popularity among many of the investors who are younger in the WallStreetBets group.

To members of the retail trading industry, it was like a hit to the back. On the surface it appeared that Robinhood wasn't "for the people" after all, but was working in conjunction with Wall Street in what appeared to be a bid to reduce losses for institutions at the expense of small men who live on Main Street. In addition, the new rules were designed to create a barrier for retailers to adopt coordinated strategies for market entry all over the world.

One exchange was extremely hot, Barstool Sports founder Dave Portnoy (a optimistic GME trader, who was reported to have was able to lose $700,000 in by trading in the shares) even went as far to refer to Robinhood the CEO Vladimir Tenev a "liar" as well as a "rat" and even suggested that members of the management of the brokerage ought to "go to jail" because of their decisions to cut off GME orders from to the long end of the marketplace.

In the end, there were no charges filed against the Robinhood management team however the CEO Tenev was later required to give evidence before U.S. Congress and answer questions regarding the reasons why the business introduced these specific restrictions on its customers. The previous statements of Robinhood has suggested that its trading restrictions required to be in accordance to SEC regulations, stating:

"These requirements exist to protect investors and the markets, and we take our responsibilities to comply with them seriously, including through the measures we have taken."

In the wake of Robinhood's decision to limit purchases of shares in GameStop this stock reverted the gains it had made prior to and plummeted from its all-time highest levels (at $483) and hit the lows that were $112.25 for each share (an overall decrease of -57.6 percent) at the close of the tense January 28th session of trading.

Similar restrictions were imposed through various other brokerages for trading that are popular (such such as Interactive Brokers).

This decision to stop trades for traders who are not retail, while the hedge funds of Wall Street were able to continue trading through their traditional platforms is what made the GameStop drama into a more modern version of David against. Goliath (and led to many accusations of market manipulation that adversely impacted the site's customers).

Jan 29th, 2021:

On the following date, Robinhood released a statement saying that its restrictions on the platform for trading stocks would be relaxed, but traders were only allowed to purchase a single part of GME (and other tickers that are on its list of restricted stocks). It should be noted that no limitations were put on the traders' rights to sell the shares that are on the restricted list of Robinhood's trading.

Before the market was set to opened on January 29 the SEC issued a statement that serves as a cautionary note to different trading brokers and Reddit users of the potential for manipulation of markets or abusive trading:

"The Commission is closely monitoring and assessing the extreme fluctuations of specific stock prices in the last few weeks... Extreme prices fluctuation has the potential of exposing investors to severe and rapid loss and undermine confidence in the market. Like always, the Commission is working to safeguard investors, and to ensure safe, stable, and efficient markets and aid in the formation of capital.

The Commission collaborates closely with its regulatory partners in the federal administration as well as FINRA and the other self-regulatory associations such as the exchanges of stocks, in order to ensure that the regulated entities adhere to their responsibilities to safeguard investors as well as to detect any potential violations. The Commission is closely reviewing any actions taken by the regulated entity which could harm investors or hinder the ability of traders to trade specific securities."

But, the market seemed to ignore the warnings of the SEC and the resurgence of buy-backs within GME led the stock to its intraday record highs at $413.98 for each share. In one session, the stock gained 68% as of the 29th January and 30th, GME stock shares GME stock posted a staggering increase that exceeded 400% in just a few days. According to research on market-tomarket conducted by S3 Partners, GameStop's short-sellers have been reportedly enduring losses of more than $20 billion within less than an entire month - despite Robinhood's attempts to ease tension and to stop Reddit's quick squeeze attack through limiting its ability to buy the shares in GME.

In a bid to not be left out, Elon Musk added the #Bitcoin hashtag on his Twitter page that same day, and the market value of the Bitcoin/USD cryptocurrency pair increased by 20percent (rising over $5,000) within one hour. Musk posted a tweet that was cryptic in the wake of the turbulent GameStop trading session. The tweet basically read:

"In retrospect, it was inevitable."

In the end, Musk's tweet appeared to be an appropriate end to an extremely turbulent trading week marked by historical changes that may change the way that the retail trader is viewed in the markets at large. The "amateur" investors found in the WallStreetBets trading platform were in a position to claim victory over hedge funds as well as institutional trading firms that overruled and affected developments in the equity market for the longest time that anyone would be able to recall.

January 31st, 2021:

Elon Musk (who is called "Papa Musk" by many of the traders who trade retail within the WallStreetBets community) was able to take the matter to his own as part of what was later to be a remarkable piece of investigative journalism from his end. To find the root of the issue, Musk invited Vlad Tenev the CEO of Robinhood to join a conference call via the Clubhouse application. The time was when anyone using access to the Clubhouse app was able to log on and join the chat. Musk's style of questioning was straight and precise. He asked questions that required to be addressed. Did Robinhood being pressured by"powers-that-be" in Wall Street to suspend buying actions for GameStop stocks? Did there exist any manipulations in the market that might suggest that the market is being manipulated in the favor by Wall Street? This is a transcript of Musk's conversation with Robinhood's CEO. Robinhood. The entire conversation can be heard here:

Elon Vlad The Impaler of the Stock.

Vlad"Hey everyone, thank you for having my company. It's great to be with everyone.

Elon: Alright, Vlad. What actually occurred? Tell us all the details.

Vlad The Vlad had hoped that you'd invite me to join to discuss the "Fluidi Paradox" since this was an extremely surreal week and weekend for me. One of the most amazing aspects is the number of folks coming out of dark to support the organization, provide advice which is why I met you this morning and I'm actually going to declare that I had downloaded Clubhouse just a few days ago, just to find out the app's features and this is my first real-life experience using the application. However, was introduced to your buddy Antonio, Elon, who gave me some great advice me, and later brought me up to your friend, Elon. Your advice was great. Then I thought, you already knew? I was told about the Clubhouse and I thought this is going to make up part of the game and I thought what the heck is going on? And here I am. I'm a firm believer in The Simulation Hypothesis.

Elon: Alright, well. Let the beans flow, Elon. What was the news the last week?

Why aren't consumers able to purchase GameStop shares? People are demanding an answer and are eager to learn the facts and the reality.

Vlad Vladimir: Okay, I'll start by providing an overview of my background. So I'm the Chief Executive of Robinhood...

Elon: Yes, we do the drill, mate. Come on...

Vlad Vlad: I'll work through it quickly. Don't worry. It's a matter of importance. Robinhood actually has a few firms. There's also an introducing broker dealer known as Robinhood Financial which is basically the application you've come to know and are awed by. It handles trades when you're one of the customers from Robinhood financial.

And then there's the clearing broker dealer Robinhood Securities, that clears and settles trades.

And then we also can also mention Robinhood Crypto which is our cryptocurrency business. Each of them is a kind of separate entities independently operated. In essence, on Wednesday the week before, we saw an unprecedented amount of volume and volume of traffic on the system. many of these meme stocks were going all over social media, and people joined Robinhood as well as lots of net-buy activities on them. We all know and Robinhood is currently top of the list in its iOS app store, and was pretty similar to, but not quite top on Google Play too. It's just an unprecedented amount of growth, don't you think? It's Thursday morning. Okay but I'm asleep, however, at 3:00am Pacific time the operations team gets an email from the NSCC which is also known as the National Securities Clearing Corporation. As the clearing broker which is also the point where Robinhood Securities comes in, we must pay funds for the NSCC according to a number of variables like the risk of trading activities, the concentration of specific securities (this is an equities-related business and it's all about the trading of stocks, not on trading in options, or something else) So they provided us a report that contained the deposit. The amount requested was about $3b which is a amount that is a lot more than the typical amount in the past, isn't it?

Elon: Why is that this high? It seems like an unimaginably high capital market demand. Which formula did they employ in calculating the amount?

Vlad Vladimir: Let's provide context for that figure Robinhood to date was able to raise around $2 billion as venture capital to this point. It's an impressive number. 3 billion dollars is certainly a significant number, surely? We aren't aware of the exact information on how the amount is calculated. It's something obscure, however there's a part called VAR (value at risk). This is based on some qualitative data, however it's still not completely transparent. There is ways to reverse engineer the formula, however it's not publically available. Additionally, there's a particular element that is a discretionary one, so it acts like an multiplier. It's essentially...

Elon: Discretionary? What do you mean by "discretionary" like it's just their personal opinion?

Vlad Vladimir: It's true that it's a small amount, but There's certainly more to it than their opinions however it's basically based on the growth of ....

Elon: What everybody wants to know is: was there a shady deal going through this time? It's a bit odd to receive an unexpected 3 billion dollars of requests at 3:30 in the early morning. Then, out of the blue.

Vlad You are right. I would not attribute some shadiness, but you're aware that the NSCC was logical following the incident and worked with us to lower the amount. It was an unprecedented act however I'm not aware of complete details about the events within the NSCC for these calculations.

Elon: Are there any people taking you hostage now?

Vlad: Uh, ha no. no. I'm OK.

Elon"Blink" twice.

Vlad Vladimir: Yeah, I know thank you for bringing it up But this is clearly nerve-racking and I had actually fallen asleep during the entire moment. Our operations team had to deal with the call at 3am, and when they returned, got our heads in order, the Chief Operating Officer of our team suggested that we call those in the upper echelons of the NSCC to find out what's happening. Perhaps there's a way that we could work together with them. There was another meeting that was lowered to around $1.4 billion dollars instead of $3. This means we're moving forward, were we not? However, it's still an extremely high percentage. Then we proposed that we explain to our clients how we control risk for these stocks all day. We also suggested that we mark these high-risk stocks as they are driving the and closing of positions only.

Then, about an hour before the market opened at 4:30 or 5:00 early in the day, they called back with the money was in deposit at $700 million. We made a deposit and then paid it promptly. Everything was in order. This is basically the reason we needed to make those symbols as closing. Also we were aware that this would be an unfavorable outcome for our the customers. The reason it was really challenging is the fact that Robinhood promotes democratizing stock market access and we're trying to provide users access to stocks, so this has been extremely difficult. However, we were forced to do so to make in this instance. We needed to comply with our regulations regarding capital and our team took everything we could to be certain that we had the resources accessible to clients.

Elon: Who is in charge of the NSCC?

Vlad the gang: It's a consortium. It's not a federal organization. I'm not really aware of what the specifics of that. To be honest I would say there was some legitimate volatility within the market. This is a rare event with meme stocks. There were a lot of transactions which suggests that there's an degree of risk added to the system, which warrants greater expectations. It's also not completely excessive. However, we implemented operational procedures to ensure that clients who had open positions were able to offer their positions for sale as a result of clearly restricting someone else, there were a lot of queries concerning "OK you had to restrict buying why didn't you also restrict selling?" And what the truth is that a lot of people become annoyed when they hold shares and wish to dispose of it, but aren't able to. This is a huge problem. There are many other brokers, I believe, were also in this same position. Then again, Robinhood was featured in news, however, you've probably heard that this was a big deal, don't you think? The other brokers also restricted exactly the same thing.

Elon: Okay, so it appears that this company will call you, and puts the power to make you and ask you to pay them or they will take it away. The main thing the people want to know is whether you make your customers pay for the trip down the river or do you simply have no other choice? If you didn't have a alternative, that's fine. Then we have to discover the reason you didn't have a choice, and also who are the people that claim you have no option?

Vlad Vlad: Yes, I'm sure that's right. It is our responsibility to meet these rules, and financial institutions also have their own requirements. These requirements are based on a formula. is a bit unclear. It would be beneficial if there was an increase in transparency in order to better plan about this. However, to be fair we did manage to provide our customers with a service in just 24 hours. Our team has raised more than one billion dollars in capital, so in the morning when we will open we'll have the ability to lower the strict limitations on position that were imposed on the securities on Friday.

Elon There will be limitations?

Vlad Vladimir: I'm sure there's going to be a theoretical limit as we don't possess infinite capital, are we? There were limits. So there's bound to be a certain limits. My concern is whether the limits will remain high enough to the level that they don't affect 99.99 percent of the customers. However, if a person were to make a deposit of 100 billion dollars and choose to exchange one stock it wouldn't be feasible.

Elon: I think people are interested in knowing who put the gun on your head ought to be accountable to the people.

Vlad Vladimir: Hey, listen to me, there are procedures, but this is atypical circumstances, and for fairness to those individuals, they've been fair. Therefore, that the only thing not being understood by people is the fact that Robinhood is an active participant in the financial system, so we are required to cooperate with all these opposition parties, so we receive a number of inquiries such as why we collaborate with market makers, and why we collaborate with clearing houses, and it's not easy to construct an introduction to an agent for clearing brokers, but and not many are doing it. The financial system which allows clients to exchange shares is an incredibly multi-layered web with multiple players and every person says it could be more efficient, and it can be enhanced, however, it's a requirement of trading in equity markets in the US which requires you to deal with all of the above.

Elon Then, in how much are you obligated to Citadel?

Vlad Vladimir: It was some rumor that Citadel or some other market makers had us pressured into this, but that's not true isn't it? Market makers are the ones who execute our trades. They perform trades for every broker, however this was a clearinghouse option, and the decision was solely based on capital demands. Our perspective is that Citadel and the other market makers were not involved in the process.

Elon: Why wouldn't the industry have a control over who is the job of leading this organization because it's an industrial consortium, is not a regulator of government?

Vlad Vlad: I'm not sure I have any basis to believe in this. I believe that's a kind of wanting to get into conspiracy theories just a bit. There's no basis to think that's true.

Elon: Ok. Alright. We'll have to be watching the outcome of any future decisions. Hope that it was helpful, and amusing. Have you been entertained?

Feb 1st, 2021:

In the midst of what could be described as an extremely turbulent and difficult month ever in GameStop's time in its public trading business, Robinhood found itself in the fullest destruction control, and was in desperate require of more funds from the various stakeholders. Within a few days, investment companies Ribbit Capital as well as Sequoia Capital secured $1 billion in financing for the zero-fee trading brokerage, another group of current shareholders (including Index Ventures, Andreessen Horowitz, ICONIQ, and NEA) have raised $2.4 billion more funding to assist in supporting Robinhood's stressed operation.

The momentum-driven buying demand for GameStop shares soared and Robinhood's platforms faced a lot of pressure because of the high trade volume and record-breaking order volumes resulting from the January events. In addition, the company was subject to increased scrutiny from politicians as well as celebrities from social media, who focused on the impression of inequity practices in trading that favor institutions over Robinhood's regular customers. In the end, Robinhood found itself having to implement a tactical plan to stem the bleeding, in line with requirements of the SEC for transparency.

Feb 2nd 2021: The 2nd of February 2021 U.S. Treasury Secretary Janet Yellen scheduled a conference along with prominent regulators of the financial sector in order to examine the recent events that affected GameStop stock, and the possible long-term implications for the market's volatility. This meeting featured key information from SEC, Federal Reserve, as well as the Commodity Futures Trading Commission (CFTC). In a press release sent to Reuters, Treasury spokeswoman Alexandra LaManna said:

"Secretary Yellen believes the integrity of markets is important and has asked for a discussion of recent volatility in financial markets and whether recent activities are consistent with investor protection and fair and efficient markets."

The gathering revealed the growing anxiety expressed at the top level of government are related to the sudden rises in the volatility of short-term stocks. This meeting was designed to speed up a review of compliance with regulatory requirements among companies that are not banks.

The focus was on the stocks that are discussed on Reddit's WallStreetBets forums The U.S. Treasury Department's examination took a close review of Citadel (and the other short selling businesses) in order to comprehend how these companies played a role in causing erratic price fluctuations and to determine how coordination of trading actions could result in a negative impact on uninitiated investors.

Feb 4th, 2021:

On February 4, Robinhood gave in to increasing pressures and lifted the restrictions on trading in a capitulation gesture that let its customers on its platform easily open large positions (of any size) within GameStop stock. As of this time, the prices in GME have returned to levels equivalent to prices that preceded the times that saw extreme volatility in trading between January 26 and February 2nd.

But, significant buying returned after Robinhood users could easily execute long-term positions. the shares of GME climb to $95 levels in the next trading session. Investors who were looking to profit on the volatility of prices in the near term profited from the power of these gains and the GME stock closed at $63.77 (with one-session gains of 19.2 percent) on February 5. The following two weeks the stock was traded in an even tighter price range (roughly $35-$60 per share) in anticipation of an upcoming event that could determine trends in the market's appraisals.

Feb 18th 2021:

The 18th of February was the day that The U.S. House Committee on Financial Services was held to hear a testimony that was titled "Game Stopped? Who Wins and Loses When Short-Sellers, Social Media, and Retail Investors Collide" In an online setting, Vlad Tenev and other important figures in the GameStop story were set to provide Congressional testimony about what would be the most famous short squeeze in GameStop shares.

The hearing was held on March 24, Vlad Tenev defended prior decision to limit trading of shares of GameStop shares and claimed that claims that Robinhood was acting to aid hedge funds and institutional investors was "absolutely false". Vlad Tenev continued by saying:

"The buying surge that occurred during the last week of January in stocks like GameStop was unprecedented, and it highlighted a number of issues that are worthy of deep analysis and discussion."

According to Tenev that his assessment of the "historic volatility" present in markets during these times has left Robinhood without a choice other than to stop trading in GME shares. In essence, platforms for trading like Robinhood have to put their funds into clearing houses until trades have been fully repaid between buyers and sellers. These actions are intended to protect against dangers in the event that a sudden market change results in massive losses prior to when trades have been fully completed.

Chapter 4: Irrational Exuberance or Something Else?

Exuberance that is not rational of the stock market isn't new. This is a phrase that's often used in the context of speculative investment to define the kind of asset or category that could be overvalued. While Alan Greenspan coined the term, Robert J. Shiller published the first book about it. Literally. Recall the definition Shiller offered in his publication of 2000. Shiller writes,

"Irrational excitement is the psychological base of a speculative bubble. I see a speculative bubble as an event that prices rises are the cause of investors' enthusiasm. This is transmitted by the psychological effect of individual to individual which in turn amplifies stories that may justify price hikes, and drawing to a greater and bigger segment of investors, who even though they doubt the importance of investing, are attracted to it because of envy at others' achievements and partly because of thrill of a gambler. (Shiller, 2000)

The stock market has experienced many balloons burst and shorts squeezed. What is unique in the GameStop report is that the euphoria among buyers wasn't irrational or simply motivated by the desire to make large profits. It was more likely to be a planned type of protest from those who were more concerned with causing damage to Wall Street than about losing their hard-earned cash to the cause (when it was bound to explode, obviously). The GameStop event was not just an exuberant irrational mania; it was the birth of a revolutionary method of challenging the status quo. Trading Populism.

Derek Thompson of The Atlantic The Atlantic wrote about the GameStop incident well. wrote:

"A ludicrous stock mania born of pandemic boredom and FOMO, piggybacking off of a clever Reddit revenge plot, which targeted hedge funds, who made a reckless bet on a struggling retailer--and it's going to end with lots of people losing incredible amounts of money." (Thompson 2021)

In various ways it is possible to see the GameStop tale can be seen as a fairy tale for the present day as a group of unnoticed marginal investors came together to fight the excess and excessiveness that have characterized that Wall Street hedge fund community since the beginning. At the end of the day, the social trading revolution of Reddit has thrown up a number of challenges to markets and reshaped the power balance to a degree that no one would have imagined in the past few days. As per David Sekera, (Morningstar's chief U.S. market strategist):

"The days of equity research limited to the large, bulge-bracket Wall Street firms is long past."

The digital democratization of the market has allowed investors (of any size account) to gain access to relevant data instantly, connect with similar social media networks and to make investment choices with the same weight and authority as big bank.

With a growing amount of investors are introduced to about the new technology, the current system of power will continue to undergo disruptions to accommodate an increase in technological democratization. Similar views were echoed in the post by Jason Wilkinson (a WallStreetBets trader who switched to

Reddit following the dismissal of his employer shortly before the onset of the epidemic):

"Some of those who participate on the WallStreetBets thread may be in line with the analysts of the hedge funds. The trick is knowing whom to pay attention to and whom to avoid. This is really a collection of people who are sharing thoughts. This is the same as Jim Cramer is on CNBC and slams buttons."

There is no doubt that some social media marketers have objectives which are different to the goals of investment for other traders. This means it is difficult to distinguish between traders who are investing in moral sanity and traders who are able to identify high-risk investments on a regular base. As per market analyst Neil Wilson, some of GameStop's Reddit traders took on an "vigilante" mindset that was focused at those who are part of the Wall Street establishment:

"They had a peculiar vigilante morality that seemed hell-bent on taking on Wall Street. They seem to hate hedge funds and threads are peppered with insults about 'boomer' money. It's a generational fight, redistributive --and all about robbing the rich to give to the millennial 'poor'."

In this instance, it is a factwithin a couple of weeks, the dominance of the realm of finance changed with a transformation that is unquestionable and completely unexpected. Because of this, it's also clear that market trading on a tactical basis across the world of equity is likely to never ever be the same.

Bi-Partisan Unity

Following the controversial decision to prohibit retail investors from buying GameStop shares as wild price swings were hitting hedge funds that held short positions in the shares Another sign of democracy and unification came in the appearance of an unanticipated bi-partisan deal to examine accusations of misconduct filed by Robinhood Markets, Inc. From the rising of the left, to the popularism on the right and vice versa, both political parties on both sides were willing to support the majority of younger generations of investors who wanted to shake up the conventional financial system and bring about an era of equity in wealth by the use of social investment.

In a highly-publicized instance, Republican Senator Ted Cruz from Texas as well as Democratic Congresswoman Alexandria Ocasio-Cortez of New York were able to reach a consensus disapproving of Robinhood and calling for an inquiry at the company's unfair imposition of limits to trading on specific segments of investors.

On Twitter, Representative Ocasio-Cortez stated that the actions of Robinhood are "unacceptable" and that further investigation into the situation are required.

"This is not acceptable. It is now time to learn more about the decision of Robinhood to stop retail investors from buying stocks, while hedge fund managers have the freedom to make trades on the stock however they choose. Being a member of the Financial Services Committee, I'd recommend a hearing in the event of need.

Investigations into freezes need to not be restricted only to Robinhood. It is a matter of serious concern. The committee investigators must look at the retail stores that freeze purchase of stock as part of investigations, particularly the ones that permit sales, however not freezing purchases."

Responding to the public request for an inquiry senator Cruz (a prominent political opponent prior to being involved in a number of fierce exchanges with Ocasio Cortez) posted a retweet of the tweet and concisely stated: "Fully agree." Practically speaking the extraordinary display of a political consensus showed legislators from all parties recognized the necessity of addressing weaknesses in the global financial system which typically favors the most powerful players.

Similar sentiments were echoed in the tweets of Republican senator Marsha Blackburn from Tennessee in response to the news via Twitter with the following tweet: "Free the traders on Robinhood." Another tweet that showed evidence of the unity among both party lines, Democratic Congresswoman Rashida Tlaib from Michigan (a prominent part of "The Squad," along with Rep. Ocasio-Cortez) reiterated her demands to investigate Robinhood's business practices, as well as the decision to limit trading in GameStop shares. Blackburn tweeted:

"This is beyond ridiculous. It's time to hold an inquiry into Robinhood's manipulation of markets. Robinhood is preventing the possibility of trade in order to safeguard Wall Street hedge funds, taking millions of dollars away from their clients to shield investors who've been using the market for an online casino for years."

While calls for greater regulation regarding Wall Street gained in momentum It quickly became apparent that the rising tide of institutional distrust was resulting due to long-standing complaints held by people who work in the investment industry for retail.

Despite the high degree of bipartisan cooperation that appears to be a part of government U.S. government, there is no reason to believe that the feelings of inequity and discontent are going to disappear in the near future. With the majority of major benchmarks for stocks trade at record highs and there is a U.S. unemployment rate remains higher, the wide gulfs among Main Street and Wall Street allow us to observe the increasing percentages of people are experiencing the sting of unfairness and anger. In light of the weakening state of the economy globally in the post-pandemic period, many experts believe that financial difficulties are likely to persist throughout the duration of.

In a lot of ways, it echoes emotions that were experienced at the time of the 2008 financial crisis (when the 10 million Americans were forced to leave their home) and it is also possible to recall that the political eras following eventually led to that Tea Party movement of the right, and to that of the left and Occupy Wall Street protests of the left. While Reddit's attack against Wall Street might not have any specific political motives from both sides, the bi-partisan initiatives that have been viewed at the top administrations reflect the true populist character of the GameStop scandal and its potential effect on the financial market. As per Republican Newt Gingrich (Speaker of the House during the Clinton administration):

"It's not all about Republicans or Democrats. It's a multitude of ordinary, normal people that began to realize that they had been cheated in this year, just as they did in 2009 and 2008. The result is an unintentional cultural response that the smaller guys and gals are forming a group and taking on the bigger players which means that the bigger players have to alter the game to keep their jobs."

The 2008 government bailout program worth $700 billion allowed for big banks to keep operating However, no of the top managers responsible for orchestrating the financial meltdown of 2008 was never prosecuted for their reckless behavior. Remaining anger fueled by public rage remained evident for over 10 years and it was in this environment in which there was a time when the Tea Party movement began to get momentum. In 2010 the Republicans won majority control over the House of Representatives while the Democrats were confronted with a backlash by progressive protestors who were concerned about the problem of inequality in economics (which eventually led to an Occupy Wall Street movement).

With the outcome that was not favorable to these events in the past It is unlikely that hedge funds that are on not on the right side of the GameStop trading will be able to get any appreciation or even sympathy from decision-makers in Washington. Today, Congress appears to be more receptive to concerns of the institutional investors who are who are on Wall Street and instead might decide to use recent events to promote popular agendas in favor of those who trade retail. Based on Republican Strategist Josh Holmes (advisor to Mitch McConnel senator of Kentucky):

"There's plenty of political currency that is holding the feet of hedge funds to the heat from Democrats as well as Republicans. If you're at Wall Street looking at this discrediting those who aren't aware of the ways market systems work I believe you're likely get into a lot of trouble."

Both on both sides The recent turmoil in the market which was triggered by the GameStop incident can be seen as a vote on the systemic elitism that has been a hallmark of Wall Street from the very beginning. The bipartisan agreement to tighten regulations and penalize long-standing ways of corporate greed are likely to be more likely based on the way Republicans as well as Democrats have confronted the restrictive policies taken by Robinhood as well as other brokerages. According to Republican Congressman Jeff Fortenberry of Nebraska:

"Big Hedge, which has outlets in South Hedge-istan (Wall Street) as well as North Hedge-i-stan (Greenwich, CT), has earned billions by shorting huge American firms that are facing a tough period of. They are now getting revenge from massive flash mobs of day traders, and they pay a hefty price."

Many moderates as well as political centrists appear to be adopting a firm stance saying there was evidence that

Robinhood (and other brokerages for trading) were involved in actions that helped institutional and hedge fund investors, at the expense of the retail trading industry. A moderate lawmaker who has taken this position can be Republican Pat Toomey (Senator from Pennsylvania) and, who is also will soon be named the chairman of the Senate Banking Committee. Senator Toomey has recently expressed his concern and pointed out the insufficient transparency after the restrictions on transactions for retail through its platform.

"I find it very troubling that consumers who are trying to purchase stocks are kept out of the market. Retail investors ought to be able to invest in even highly speculational shares, the same way hedge funds are free to trade their shares."

The Cryptocurrency Connection

In the wake of the January 28th the 2021 session of trading (which was the day the time when GME stock shot up to record-setting highs at $483.08 per share) markets for assets that are crypto-related began to witness another increase in the buying of. In particular, the value of bitcoin against that of the U.S. dollar (represented by the crypto pair BTC-USD) has reversed from its previous lower levels (near $32,000) and started to rise through the remainder of the month. On the 21st of February, prices for BTC-USD jumped up to new records (just less than $58,400) with an increase of more than 93% within three and a half months.

To provide a benchmark for reference, the main U.S. stock benchmark (S&P 500) decreased by -3.2 percentage during the time and this deterioration suggests that bitcoin's valuation was capable of overcoming the predominant bearish trend observed across the vast majority markets. But this purchasing activity wasn't limited only to bitcoin, as strong uptrends could be seen across the major altcoins of the cryptocurrency market. Market valuations, for instance, for Ethereum rose up to 67.3 percentage during this time (as shown by the ETH/USD currency pair). This shows that the cryptocurrency optimism goes far beyond bitcoin when it comes to its ability to penetrate market that is digitally democratic.

It is true that bitcoin and Ethereum are both names that are well-known to investors who do not have exposure to cryptocurrency It shouldn't be a surprise to see these currencies rise or fall in any given day. But, the Binance coin (represented by the BNB-USD crypto pair) witnessed bullish movements which were more significant and a lot more pronounced. Particularly, the BNB-USD pair was up by more than 760percent during the trading period which ran from January 28th through the 19th of February, so the moves managed surpass all of the widely well-publicized bullishness on bitcoin market that was being announced at the time.

The lesser-known altcoins also benefited from the retail-based trading optimism which accompanied the initial development of the GameStop story. An additional example can be seen on Cardano (represented in the ADA-USD crypto pairs) and has risen by 385% over the course of a month following the highest levels in GME stocks. In addition it was noted that there was a rise in the Litecoin cryptocurrency (represented by the crypto pair) overcame bitcoin's growth (with the gains between January and February 2021 of 104 percent) as well as the popular polka dot currency saw gains of 182 percentage (more than double the gain of bitcoin in this time period).

In the majority of cases, the impressive rally was not covered in the Financial news media and it could have been because Wall Street's analysts were taken by surprise by the news of the shocking report in GameStop. A deeper dive into the key developments that were taking place in the midst of this time indicates that retail traders' ability to alter the perception of Wall Street towards the social aspect of trading and investment democracy was much more than just a couple of popular stocks that were mentioned in the r/WallStreetBets group.

"For this reason there is a rising number of market experts have begun to argue that there's an unspoken connection between GameStop's recent changes and increasing valuations of the cryptocurrency market.

Particularly, the enormous disdain for central finance in the way is typically used by government agencies is only adding pressure to the rapid use of crypto."

Naturally, a lot of these views are to be rooted in the fundamental characteristics that define the core utilities of cryptocurrency in the market open.

Many times, those who have more of trading on market for financial instruments are more prone to taking in the occurrences that become evident in a variety of categories of asset. Because of this, the discussion of democratizing investment in the GameStop report is noteworthy since it can be compared to a story in the market for cryptocurrency which occurred a brief period of time before.

At the close of the month of December, 2020 market valuations for BTC-USD climbed to hit record-breaking levels barely below $25,000. Three weeks later, these valuations soared to more than 72 percent (reaching levels just under $42,000 on January 8 2021) And many of these market rallies that were bullish were caused by the growing recognition of crypto as a durable storage of value.

In a way, it is a novel form of currency that is digital Bitcoin is held digitally with no need to have external oversight from any external entity. Bitcoins cannot be printed the same way as fiat currency can be printed. This type of digital transactions has usher into a new age of financial markets that could have resulted in one of the major investment revolutions of time. One of the main characteristics of the cryptocurrency market is that the assets of bitcoin are not centralized that is, in fact, one major difference in comparison to traditional fiat currencies. Because no institution or government manages the bitcoin network The democratization and protection which is the hallmark of bitcoin has left numerous investors at ease since the banks of the world will not have control over the price of bitcoins.

In light of these factors, it's not an unwelcome surprise that bitcoin first came to existence within the period following the financial crisis of 2008. Following the 2008 financial crisis, Lehman Brothers unexpectedly filed for the biggest bankruptcy ever and the public's confidence in big banks was shattered and the government's actions to help several of the major actors responsible for what eventually turned out to be the credit crunch stoked fears of loss of trust among individuals who invested. In the early days, the web's top social media sites were still with forms that were not developed, and that resulted in retail investors having very few avenues for communicating and debate new ideas in trading.

Peer-to-peer technology in Bitcoin has helped address a variety of issues as well as the anonymity of the transactions create a sense of security which individual investors previously not had. Bitcoin users can hold several wallets (each each with a unique bitcoin account) and not have to sign up names, residence addresses or any other kinds of data that are associated with personal identification. In addition, this anonymity is accompanied by an extremely high degree of transparency due to the fact that each bitcoin transaction is stored on the network (the vast general ledger referred to in the world of blockchain). In addition, investors of all kinds have the ability to enjoy these advantages by paying very little trading charges since the concept of an intermediary "middleman" has become largely out of date. Prior to the advent of cryptocurrency, foreign transactions could have been costly. In the present digital currency framework, all transactions are free of borders and the requirement to carry out money transactions via a set of connected banking institutions could become outdated and should be put in the trash of the past.

The majority of cryptocurrency traders, these benefits have been evident as bitcoin started trading on the market. It has however taken some time for the investment group to accept these concepts and recognize the real benefits of cryptocurrency assets. Some famous examples are Warren Buffett's assessment Bitcoin as "rat poison squared," that was followed by warnings for investors not to buy the currency. Similar views were also expressed in the words of Jamie Dimon (CEO of JPMorgan) in his statement that bitcoin was "a fraud" which creates risk for investors that is "worse than tulip bulbs."

In this instance, it must be noted that there could not be any confusion regarding the remarks of Mr. Dimon's statements since he backed off and clarified his negative opinion in his statement the JPMorgan traders contemplating long-term bitcoin positions:

"I would fire them in a second, for two reasons: It is against our rules and they are stupid --and both are dangerous."

Maybe not the most lucid (or convincing) arguments for investing that have ever been offered, the pervasive disdain of one of the biggest changes in the development of finance being "stupid" goes far beyond being unable to hold an informed debate about the subject that was, in truth, may be a contentious issue back then. Particularly, the reluctance to acknowledge the possibility of digitalization in the world's currency markets could have initially dissuaded investors from taking part in some of the largest market rallies of the past.

In the year Jamie Dimon made his misguided and misinformed assertions about bitcoin being useful for people with criminal motives, BTC-USD traded for less than $4500, and the subsequent rallies a few days later affirm the untruthfulness of institutions' inability to acknowledge the advantages of cryptocurrency assets. For those who aren't sure about the details of Mr. Dimon's arguments and arguments, here's a different gem that cryptocurrency investors should take into consideration:

"If you were in Venezuela or Ecuador or North Korea or a bunch of parts like that, or if you were a drug dealer, a murderer, stuff like that, you are better off doing it in bitcoin than U.S. dollars... So, there may be a market for that, but it would be a limited market."

Contrary to statements that cryptos cannot exist outside of the confines of a "limited market," the market value of bitcoin surpassed $1 trillion mark at the beginning of 2021. In terms of a comparable metric we must recognize that the value of bitcoin surpassed the entire market value that was held by JPMorgan, Citi, and Bank of America combined during the exact same time. If we say that this kind of comparative improvement in the financial market can be viewed as a valid way to punish JPMorgan Chief Executive Officer Jaimie Dimon is an understatement. From 2018 onwards, it's evident that bitcoin has had moments of weakness, however the rising valuations for BTC-USD as we've witnessed recently show that the volatility of cryptocurrency is centered around the positive direction.

In contrast the traditional asset classes (i.e. securities in the financial industry) are in a state of failure, which could offer investors an justification for the reason JPMorgan has announced the launch of its own cryptocurrency in 2019. If you are unable to compete with them, take a page from them or just follow the trading industry of retail with a less well-known coin offering, which isn't able to attract global investors significantly. In the end, this turn of the fortunes of cryptocurrency traders should leave them with some measure of assurance that their strategies for investing could never be regarded by the media as "rat poison" that would make more sense as "buying tulips in the 17th century."

However, if the asset's harshest critics are being part of the revolution the cryptocurrency traders must have done something correct, and it's evident that their decisions have paid off with a rate that is higher than those of the other assets present in the financial markets. The overall trend is that previous efforts to block cryptocurrency investments with criticism and dismissal have been unsuccessful in the end, and the power of the established market seems to diminish rather fast. The historical price charts of Bitcoin are clear enough and it's hard to argue convincingly for the traditional stock market (especially ones that are that are in the financial sector) in a market where they lose in such large amounts.

Essentially, when people seek out reasons to understand why cryptocurrency-skeptics have altered their views on bitcoin, and the other digital currencies and digital assets, the solution appears to be straightforward that they had the option of not having. In the present, it's evident that the current situation has led to Jamie Dimon and the "Oracle of Omaha" appear to be misinformed because of the enormous possibility of gains, which has been ignored because of what could be described as illogical justifications. But this "expert" dismissals appear to not have affected the confidence of the investment retail crowd to purchase cryptocurrency. In the end, the overall upward trend in BTC-USD's bullishness during the period preceding the GameStop short squeeze shows that it won't remain the responsibility of traditional institutions to judge the worth of cryptocurrency. investments will keep generating significant gains in the future.

However, there's an abundance of research that indicates that institutions' investment in cryptocurrency has begun to grow rapidly. While these bigger "establishment" players were clearly not up to speed however, recent changes to the bearish sentiment among the group could be the catalyst for the possibility of future short squeezes taking place within a brand different market (the crypto space). But, these kinds of incidents are not likely to take place in the near term since the investment community of institutional investors has taken a inspiration from the retail traders who were among the first buyers of crypto.

When the Reddit uprising in opposition to Wall Street hedge funds had begun to be seen in stocks like GameStop and GameStop, the market's valuations for bitcoin were already experiencing gains up to 300% over the preceding three months. If taken in conjunction in conjunction with each other, of these indicators suggest that a significant changes were taking place in different markets. The price increases that were bullish began when all three principal U.S. stock benchmarks were close to record-highs. One could argue that the apparent gap between the heightened valuations of earnings and price at Wall Street weakened labor markets and the economy on Main Street left many retail traders in a predicament which required decisive move. If this is the case and it is also claimed that the huge rises on bitcoin were a prelude to the developments that would happen in market prices (i.e. the shares in GameStop) within a couple of months afterwards.

In every way trading professionals who want to study how long-term effects will be impacted by the Reddit Rebellion must understand that such events do not occur on their own. The bullish movement towards social trading as well as the increasing democratization of investing was 10 years in the making. There are clear indications of the social trading trends that would lead to the GameStop scandal could be spotted before the time, and the primary reason of this is the evidence that the trading community was generally disdainful of their "advice" of some of famous people in the Wall Street establishment (i.e. Jamie Dimon and Warren Buffett and many other people).

The political establishment is on its side (and demanded investigations into the conduct of brokerages such as Robinhood) This suggests that there's not much backing in the direction of Wall Street hedge funds or the investment industry that is dominated by institutions. If this trend continues and continue, it is like this weakened segment of the market is required to bow in the favor of the trading community on social media. In certain ways, this may be a sign that we will see an increasing amount of investments from hedge funds bitcoin and other crypto currencies. The result of the squeeze that was initiated by the community r/WallStreetBets shows that the market for equity is no longer safe in the direction of the democratization of markets.

A scenario that may drastically change this optimistic outlook could be when Congress begins to consider stricter regulations for the cryptocurrency market. It's a possibility to keep at the forefront of anyone who would like to put actual money into any of these markets as the risk of losing should not be ignored for traders of any kind (short-term or longer-term). So far, we've witnessed little unambiguous statements by government officials which seem focused on enforcing stricter regulations for the cryptocurrency market. But that doesn't not mean these kinds of incidents won't occur in the near future. In fact, based on the way U.S. politicians (from both side of the aisle) have indicated their an endorsement for the community of retail traders and the retail trading community, it is clear the precedent that was set. All it means is that social trading will be a more the investment of people rather than hedge funds that are based on Wall Street and the institutional investing group.

It is crucial for investors to comprehend the practicality of the role that cryptocurrency plays in the investment portfolio as well as in daily commercial transactions. Bitcoin, at its heart (like numerous other cryptocurrency) operates on a network designed as a fully functional digital currency which is completely independent of any central authority. There's no centralized authority or central bank who is thought to be responsible for these transactions due to bitcoin's peer-to-peer system that allows transactions in financial terms to be conducted between the users (while keeping their identities private) without the need for intermediaries.

Bitcoin transactions operate by utilizing a system of nodes which are protected by encryption and permit crucial process of verification to occur. The transactions themselves are recorded on an open ledger (a blockchain) that is available to all and enables users in securing themselves from threats of hacking or theft, as well as fraud without relying on private security systems. Bitcoins are exchangeable in exchange for services, goods and fiat currencies, as well as any other cryptocurrency. Bitcoins can be created by the "mining" process (compiling bitcoin transaction data into the ledger of public record) which further reward those who allow this process to be decentralized in its place.

In the year 2020, the amount of bitcoin users who are active surpassed 432,000 "active entities," which is defined as the collection of wallets owned by single user who has conducted an Bitcoin transactions (sending and receiving) in a 24 hour period. This figure is basically telling us how many users who use bitcoin frequently and it is steadily increasing from the start of 2018. Based on Matthew Dibb, founding member of Stack (a firm that offers price tracking for cryptocurrency and crypto index fund):

"While this metric has reached levels not seen since last year however, it's done it slowly, without the 'bubble-like' increase. We are reassured by this by comparing clusters of addresses with future-oriented price movements."

In the end, Matthew Dibb is suggesting that the price of bitcoin tends to rise as the amount of users who are regular grows. Based on the demand-supply patterns that are the basis of the modern theory of economics and practice, it should not come as shocking since widespread acceptance of crypto currencies tends to boost market demand, which could result in the valuation of prices to increase as time passes. Based on Business Insider, roughly 106 million individuals around the globe used cryptocurrency as of January 20, 2021. Additionally, a increasing number of people of those in the Baby Boomer and Generation X population expressed curiosity about using cryptocurrency.

An identical study by DeVere (a business that offers financial advisory services) discovered that more than three quarters of clients who were over the age of 55 been involved in investing at least once in a cryptocurrency or planned to invest in it by 2021. While the usage of bitcoin as well as other crypto currencies tends to be thought to be associated with younger buyers (mainly people who fall within the Millennial age range) Recent data indicate that this isn't true. It is evident that the fact is that the use of cryptocurrency has become increasing commonplace across every age group and the constant, increasing use of cryptocurrency is likely to push bitcoin prices upwards over time.

Naturally, bitcoin is also being criticized for its potential the use of illegal transactions, its fluctuating price and large quantities of energy utilized by crypto miners. Some in the world of financial analysis are of the opinion that bitcoin could be an unrealized bubble, which may cause financial harm to investors in the event of an economic crash within the next few years. Naturally, these kinds of incidents are a real possibility should we witness government organizations as well as central banks across the globe calling for a stricter regulation of the use of crypto-assets. But, the reality that these kinds of investments were able to rise in popularity at beginning demonstrates that there is a growing demand for alternatives to fiat currencies and that is the reason for the recent introduction of cryptocurrency assets on the world market is a major occasion.

It is not difficult to conclude that there are a variety of macroeconomic variables that have led to the rapid growth of Bitcoin and the rise of decentralized trading. For instance, in the United States, government debt is on the rise for a long time and the ratio of GDP to debt (which is a measure of total debt in relation with annualized economic output) is at (or over) 100% from 2013. Most experts view this 100 percent limit as a possible danger zone, and when debt is higher than the output of the nation typically, this is an indication that a economic crisis is fast nearing. If global investors start to doubt the capacity to trust government officials of the United States government to meet its obligations to repay debt Financial analysts could begin to suggest it is possible that it is possible that the U.S. dollar is on the edge of being devalued as the primary currency in the world. As per Financial Times columnist Rana Foroohar:

"The increase in the the popularity of volatile cryptocurrency such as bitcoin might appear to be a possible indicator of this Federal Reserve-powered foam. It could also be seen as a indication of a future global order, in which the US as well as the dollar be less influential."

In ways that seem alarmingly similar to many other nations that are experiencing declining around the globe and the United States seems to show no interest in reverseing the dangerous trends caused by its increasing deficits. Furthermore, budgetary indicators across the globe seem to indicate that many central banks will keep printing funds at alarming rates, regardless of when the COVID-19 outbreak is over, but the majority of these quantitative easing initiatives will likely be tiny compared to policies that have been introduced from Federal Reserve officials. Federal Reserve.

In the end, these macroeconomic trends that are not sustainable seem to suggest that a change in the economy is expected to happen in the fiat currency market (and on the basis of the U.S. dollar, in particular). It's the kind of situation that will allow bitcoin to increase in value as global investors keep looking at alternatives to market for digital currencies. A lot of small-scale businesses have began using cryptocurrency for transacting international business which is especially relevant in nations where it is difficult to obtain U.S. dollars (i.e. Nigeria) or in countries where high price inflation of currencies has caused unstable conditions in the overall economy (i.e. Argentina).

Bitcoin is also growing as a substitute in place of that of the U.S. dollar within consumer stores as the primary method of exchange in retail stores. Recent news reports show that Musk's electric car firm Tesla, Inc. has purchased a significant amount of bitcoin and has announced plans to take bitcoin as a method of payment for their products. This is in line with announcements by PayPal and Venmo which have announced plans to allow cryptocurrency in transactions made online. This implies that a greater percentage of transactions on the internet are likely to be made using cryptocurrency as a method of transactions. This means that while the majority of bitcoin transactions are made as a means of investment (rather than buying everyday goods or paying for bills) however, the general trend is likely to change. changing.Although certain skeptics may argue that the recent rise in Bitcoin's valuations may become an irresponsible market, the growing demand for cryptocurrency could be a significant signal to central banks prepared to print money with a high rate. Naturally, this is especially true for the United States, and the Federal Reserve should not assume that its status as a reserve currency is an absolute fact as well as that currencies based on fiat are going to be considered a good asset in the near future. For both consumers and investors the cryptocurrency market has been considered to have a higher amount of trust. It is highly likely that technologically-savvy consumers are still seeking alternatives to fiat currencies as long as they find one (or created).

The latest evidence indicates that something is obvious: cryptos have risen as a brand new category of assets that is an impressive alternative to the standard asset store that is available through the U.S. dollar. The majority of them are not governed by state agencies We can observe that the peer-to–peer networks connected to cryptocurrency are seeing a substantial increase in popularity and recognition as democratic, non-centralized investment instruments with functional applications designed for daily use. However it is that the COVID-19 disease has bolstered the views of these people (at the international level) and made bitcoin sound more than "digital hype" and more an alternative that is viable for fiat currencies, which have distinct structural flaws.

In the end, the rise of bitcoin can be seen as both the result of and manifestation of the long-term problems in economics that have been brewing for a number of decades -- issues that were masked by the loose monetary policies (low prices for interest) as well as artificially inflating price of assets that grew due to an accumulation of credit, and the application of leverage to finance market investment. These are exactly the kind of things that caused the financial crisis of 2008 and hyper-inflation in Weimar Republic, and many other financial catastrophes across the world due to the fact that, at the end there are just three methods to limit overly high debt levels such as austerity, organic growth or printing fiat currency through loose money policy.

In the event that governments across the globe continue to print fiat currency and are unable to stop the general trend in international markets, it's likely that recent surges in the bitcoin market will continue to increase in intensity and cryptocurrency (as an asset category) could gain more acceptance as a safe storage of value. In light of this favorable prospects for the future potential of cryptocurrencies It is crucial for investors to possess an accurate understanding of different instruments that are beginning growing in recognition in the market conditions. The characteristics of cryptocurrency are often unique which are distinct from each other. These significant differences could have a major impact on the future of investing in cryptocurrency and the impact it has on purchases.

As of now, the majority of people are aware of bitcoin. But they could not be as familiar with the other coins (or altcoins) as well within the category. Ethereum may be the most well-known altcoin (based on market value) as well as many of its core principles (i.e. distributed ledgers and cryptography) have a lot in common with bitcoin's operation. However, there are significant differences between the two networks. In particular, Ethereum transactions can include executable code. However, the bitcoin transaction data transactions are typically utilized for basic records and notes.

In the first place, it must be observed that the algorithms which are used to run every network transaction differ for transactions that use Ethereum. Bitcoin transactions operate according to an algorithm known as the "SHA-256" algorithm while Ethereum transactions are based on the "ethash" mining algorithm. The other major difference is the length of time needed for transactions across every network. With bitcoin, transactions can be confirmed within minutes, whereas

Ethereum transactions may only take an interval of a few minutes. To be practical, both buyers and investors must know that the two platforms have two fundamentally distinct goals.

In particular, it was developed to function as a value-store alternative to fiat currency, and serve as a means of exchange on open markets. Ethereum's platform on the side, was created to send fixed contracts and unchangeable software that could be managed with its own crypto-payment system (using the Ethereum cryptocurrency). Both Ethereum as well as bitcoin were created to allow the use of digital currencies. But, the functionality of ether wasn't designed to create an monetary system which functioned independently of international fiat currencies. The purpose of ether was to generate revenue and support the usage of decentralized apps (dapp) as well as smart contracts, which are operated through the platform.

In essence, Ethereum works as a application for a blockchain that is compatible with bitcoin, and thus it shouldn't be thought of as an BTC rival. But, ETH has held the second place (in the terms of market value) during the majority of its trading time on the marketplace, however its network is only one-fifth larger than bitcoin (as as of March 20, 2021, the market value for Ethereum was just under $ 200 billion).

Contrary in contrast to Ethereum The XRP cryptocurrency is mostly regarded as a payment system that is digital. In particular, XRP (designed by Ripple Labs) is used for investment exchange, payment settlement, as well as a remittance method (similar like SWIFT). Nowadays, many people have probably heard of SWIFT as a means of sending money internationally which rely on a network of banks and financial intermediaries organizations to finish every transaction. Instead of implementing an algorithm for mining blockchains in the XRP network, the XRP network rely on distributed consensus software that operate on servers on the platform. In essence, the Ripple platform is able to conduct a poll. Servers on the network calculate the consensus results to confirm every transaction.

This process allows to allow XRP transactions to be validated within a short amount of time, without the need to conduct additional checks that are carried out by a central authority. In the end, this lets XRP to continue its position as a cryptocurrency that is decentralized and process transactions with a speeds that are much higher than other rivals in the space of cryptocurrency. In addition it is worth noting that the Ripple platform usually requires less energy than other systems used for bitcoin transactions, since there's no mining platform for every coin. While bitcoin transactions may require several hours to get to the stage of confirmation markets transactions made that use the cryptocurrency XRP can be verified in two seconds, and at charges that are very small when compared to other assets in its class.

For market share There are 100 billion coins (all of that are pre-mined) which is more than the entire amount of bitcoin (at 21 million). This is due to the fact is that XRP coins are mined prior to being used implies that Ripple creates currency with processes that are very different as compared to bitcoin's mining mechanism (which is basically a proof-of-work method). When mining miners locate bitcoin in it, they create a brand new currency is created and added to the system. But, the new release of XRP coins are controlled by smart contracts, which are able to run at any moment. In the beginning, Ripple designed the system to allow for a certain amount of coins XRP each year (1 billion) and today, circulation of XRP has surpassed 50 billion coin. Each month, the unutilized portion of XRP coins will be deposited to an escrow account. This process is intended to prevent abuse and the oversupply of Ripple tokens. It also indicates that it could be several years before all the quantity of XRP is readily available.

The primary use of XRP is to transfer funds, however many retailers are now accepting transactions through using the Ripple platform (similar to bitcoin). Every time a transaction gets confirmed through Ripple's platform Ripple platform, a modest cost (denominated as XRP) is taken out of the account of the user. Users can be business-related or an individual, but it is it apparent that Ripple is most popular among banks. Ripple platform is particularly popular for banks. This may not come as a surprise, considering the many similarities with respect to SWIFT payment system that are used for international transactions. This is why XRP has experienced a tremendous increase due to its usage by financial institutions, and the ease of use for payment systems used in international transactions is the main benefit when contrasted with other currencies within the crypto space.

Litecoin is another well-known cryptocurrency but the scale is a tiny part of the bitcoin market. At the time of writing the market capitalization of Litecoin is approximately $13.5 billion (which is just 1.5 percentage of the bitcoin market value in the same time). Litecoin is even less valuable to the overall market value of Ethereum however, it must be noted that it took just a couple of years for bitcoin to reach the threshold of $10 billion. In essence, this indicates the fact that Litecoin assets have reached the level of worth which is very respectable and has seen substantial growth in the past couple of years.

Beyond its size, it is also a lot bigger than the Litecoin payment platform also has distinct differences in how it's distributed across the marketplace. It is interesting to note that the Litecoin platform has the capacity to hold up to an 84 million coin collection (which is more than four times the amount of bitcoins which will ultimately be made available to users). But it's not completely clear how this could influence the price of the cryptocurrency over time, as every Litecoin can be infinitely divided (similar as bitcoin). This means that Litecoin users can use the currency to conduct smaller transactions and payments as well, which means there's an extremely high degree of value that could be associated with the currency.

In its beginning when it was first introduced, the Litecoin payment system was created to facilitate fast transactions and, when we compare it with the bitcoin system, it is apparent that those goals have been accomplished. Particularly, the typical transaction confirmation timeframe for transactions made on the Litecoin platform is a little under three minutes. This is the exact amount of time required for every block to be confirmed before being added into the ledger of public transactions.

Chapter 5: Shorting

If a trader in stocks believes that a company's price dropping, they may trade shares of the company short. The process involves borrowing shares in order in order to sell them immediately or, in other words, the shares you sell don't belong to you. This is a brief outline of how it works

1.) The borrowing of shares: To start, you need to take out a loan to borrow shares. If you borrow shares then, the value of the shares you borrowed them at represents your price base. For example, suppose that you take out a loan of 100 shares of AMC Theaters (NYSE: AMC) even though the company's trading at $4 per share.

2.) Sell Shares When you've got 100 shares in AMC You then decide to offer them for sale at $4 per share. The process is typically carried out in conjunction to the previous process. In the present, you're owed 100 shares. That implies that in order to complete your trade, you'll need to acquire 100 shares. But, you've received 4 cents per share, or the total of $400, to sell the shares.

3.) buying back shares If you are a short seller expect an increase in the price of the shares you have sold. If you sell AMC short for $4 per share, but the price decreases to $2 per share and you are capable of making a 200 profit by buying 100 shares at that price, and then returning them at the loan. But, if the value increases to $14 per share, then you'll lose the money because you will have to buy the shares at a higher cost.

4.) Returning the shares: After you've repurchased shares, the position is closed out as they're given back to the person who that you took the shares from. For calculating your profit or loss, simply subtract the amount you earned when selling your shares ($4) and subtract the cost of the purchase ($14 one share). In this case, you'd lose $10 for each share ($4 $114 equals $10) which is a $1000 loss, considering that you purchased 100 shares. That's right, the 4 percent credit when you first sold shares implies that you will need the $10 you earn per share to purchase the shares at a more expensive value. This is typically performed in conjunction with step 2 above.

All in all, you're buying stocks backwards. In this regard, be aware that gains from buying stock from the company is basically unlimited and there's no limit for how high a single stock could go. However losing money from selling an investment are unlimitable and, as such, there's no limit to the heights that each stock could reach. Although this is a beneficial option for those who are buying shares, it's also an obstacle to the short-selling industry which is the root of every risks.

Brokers, naturally, know the risks associated with selling shares. Any person can be a victim of this risk. will be a price for stocks at which they'll be practically in a position of not "covering" their position (buying back shares).

Therefore, shorting shares comes with the risk of a "margin requirement" and the possibility of "margin call." What it means is that you have to keep a certain amount of liquidity or a the balance of your cash account. Regulation T imposes an upper limit of at minimum 150% of your amount of the short-term position. Therefore, if you were to sell AMC at a price of $4 per share, which is what happens in the instance in the above example, you'd be required to open with $2 per share in order to take care of the potential upside risk ($4.00 150 percent equals $6.00. Because you're credited with an initial fee of $4 when you open your trade, all you need is an additional $2 in order to meet the minimum requirement of $6).

When the account is open the maintenance requirements change to 100 percent of the value of the sale, plus 25 percent of the value of the investment. If the value of the stock rises to $8 a share, you'll require the funds of $800 for 100 shares. You will also need an additional $200 to meet the margin requirements ($800 25 percent = $200). This $1000 ($800 plus $200) is considerably more than the $600 that which you started with.

If you had $200 at the time you started the account ($600 when the proceeds of the short sale have landed in your account) If the price increases to $8 per share, you'll receive the margin call, and you will have to transfer more money promptly. In some instances the broker could be able to liquidate or sell any other position you're in to meet the cost of margin on the account.

One other thing to be aware of is the fact that Regulation T margin requirements are minimal. Some brokers charge maintenance fees that are 30%, or 40 percentage. In addition, for specific securities that are deemed to be more risky, brokers might not permit short-selling or charge maintenance fees close to 100 percent.

Every one of these small nuances can lead to the creation of having investors in the process of shorting stocks are ordered to purchase it with a larger price due to the fact that they aren't able to meet minimum margin requirements. The most feared short squeeze.

Although retail brokerages do not like trading stocks in shorts because of the potential risk hedge funds as well as short-selling businesses employ this tactic significantly more often. Therefore, prior to digging deeper into the reason they targeted GameStop particularly we'll take a moment to look at the actual actions they take.

Hedge Funds + Short Sellers

The discussion about GameStop as well as the various other squeezes that occurred at the beginning of January 2021, are awash in references to hedge funds. However, what exactly is an actual hedge fund?

In simple terms, a hedge fund is a run investment vehicle that is based on certain strategies designed to increase the returns of the fund's investors. Occasionally it is "absolute returns," while sometimes, it's "relative returns3."

Absolute returns are assessed in relation to the amount an index of the overall market returns whether or not the overall market is able to return 15% or is down by 15 percent, the company seeks to earn an increase in the clients it serves. To determine what exactly the market's overall performance is, investors typically set their sights on an individual "benchmark" that they believe will have a risk profile similar that is similar to the way they invest. Although this may be an exact index however, we'll use as an example the S&P 500 as an example since it's typically seen as an overall perspective of the economy that is the US and therefore frequently employed as a broad source of information by investors4.

However the relative return is a priority in generating "alpha," or simply beating the market. For instance, if the S&P 500 produces 15% or more, then the company would like to beat the 20% mark, for instance while, If the S&P 500 losses 15%

of its value, then the business is looking to make less losses than 10 percent. The benchmark that the hedge fund has to compare itself with can be different depending on whether they have any reference point or not. Alpha is measured by the what return the company generates over that. Below, you will find an example of two funds which have achieved either relative or absolute results. However, simply the fact that a fund is striving to achieve one of these objectives does not mean it will succeed in accomplishing it.

Most hedge funds seek to just make money regardless of the current market situation. Thus they're seeking the absolute return.

In that regard it is likely to be some common aspects of the way hedge funds work:

Gain access to more Advanced Financial Instruments A majority of funds make use of leverage, options as well as short selling, to boost yields and lower the risk

Management Fees that are High: Due to the heightened focus paid to the money managed by funds, many fund managers have greater fees. such as "2 and 20." In this case, "2" represents the amount of assets that the fund is charged, and "20" represents the percent of gain over a prior large titak which the fund is charged.

Incomplete Transparency: In contrast to mutual funds, hedge funds come with significantly obscure disclosure rules.

Although hedge funds differ greatly in their strategies One of the earliest strategies is"long/short. "long/short." There are numerous variations on this kind of strategy however, we'll simplify it by focusing only on one specific variant, called the "pair trade."

The pair trade involves the recognition of two stocks. one that it is one that the fund "bullish" on, or believes is rising. The second company is one the fund considers "bearish" on, or thinks will fall.

In most cases, these companies are grouped together into a particular sector. Take, for instance, United Airlines (NYSE: UAL) as well as American Airlines (NYSE: AAL). If a company is positive about UAL and negative on AAL, they'll "long," or purchase shares of UAL as well as short AAL. In a sense it is like they're "hedged" against sector movements. It is possible that the performance of this fund will be positive, even when markets are dipping in the manner described in the following.

This is because, if the airline sector is valued to increase They are betting on UAL growing higher than AAL. This means their long-term position will pay more than their short one. In contrast in the event that the industry is down, they anticipate AAL to decline more than UAL which means that the gains from their short investment can more than compensate for the loss on their long. Keep in mind that because the fund has a short position in AAL, each percent decline is an increase in the value of the fund. When you examine the graph below, be aware that, even though the movements downwards of AAL and UAL are similar, AAL is worth less per share. Therefore, per share, it's likely to see a larger loss.

It's as balancing act. Because the returns are the sum of its most and least players, if you short the most shaky players, and seeking out the most successful players, you are likely to earn decent profits regardless of the market's situations. This example is a somewhat simplified one and does not take into account the nuance of the situation, but it does convey certain of the most important concepts regarding the strategy.

We picked the case of American Airlines above because it was one of the stocks short squeezed in the month of January. It's because the pair trade is an atypical strategy employed by a variety of hedge funds. AAL is the most popular choice for an "bad airline." At the beginning of January 68.1 million shares of 69.75 million shares in circulation were short-sold. The theory is that it's an excellent method. When you begin seeing shares shorted at this point the situation becomes more alarming; in the near future we'll discuss the reasons how it's a ticking bomb.

When hedge funds utilize this method, some companies called short-selling companies for example Citron Research, typically have short-term positions in place and even can even provide research on the difficulties that they face with the stocks they are selling. While many view them with a negative view because of this however, this isn't necessarily illegal it can be extremely profitable6. The market usually rewards the ones who be more risky over others, which happens with some short-selling companies. But in January we were able to see the ramifications of this choice by them. The market is quick to respond, but sometimes it takes quicker, especially if risks are not taken into account.

In order to make the idea, Citron clocked in such massive losses that they are no longer a short-term firm. in the future it will be betting on stock prices rising, not going down.

Shorting GameStop

Chapter 6: Enter GameStop NYSE GME

If you're not aware, GameStop is an American retailer which sells video games consoles, games and accessories. The company has faced stress for a long time due to the growth of online commerce and the move away from brick and mortar shops.

If you have an Xbox or PS4 You know you don't need move from your seat for a purchase You just need the credit card number of your parents number, and an internet connection then a new game on video is in your reach. The COVID-19 virus just served to increase this trend. It led to mall closings as well as a general shifting away from online buying forcing the company into the brink of the brink of bankruptcy.

There was blood everywhere Bets were made against the business. Certain companies, like Citron Research, just traded short while other were able to pairs trades. As an example, companies like Melvin Capital shorted GameStop while looking for firms such as Unity Software, a video game development company7. The other companies that participated in similar pair trades included D1 Capital Partners and Mapleplan. Candlestick employed the short/long strategy that is available on GameStop but it was not an directly related pair of trades.

While there were plenty of money looking to place bets against the firm There were those that were prepared to disbelieve the company's view and put their money into the company's stock. Companies such as Scion Capital, run by Michael Burry, the famous Michael Burry, went long by buying more than two million shares (though the stake was eventually cut by 1.7 million shares)8. It was Dr. Burry rightly believed that GameStop could have huge potential for upside due to the launch of brand new consoles, video games in franchises that had been proven and the internal drive to meet the shift from analog to digital. (The origin of this data isn't mentioned here and can be found from the 13F's of the firm, accessible on the website of the SEC.)

A little less one, the popular Redditor, u/DeepFuckingValue, took on place on GME in the year 2019 using shares9 and calls. shares9. The person that was behind the username is Keith Gill, a Chartered Financial Analyst (CFA) who was employed for Mass Mutual Life Insurance up till recently. He started buying on June 7 in 2019 and with calls of $8 which expire on the 15th of January 2021. Talk about the timing.

Keith has shared his findings both in Wall Street Bets and his YouTube channel, Roaring Kitty10. The former is greater in the context than the other; Wall Street Bets, known through its abbreviation, r/WSB was to become the place of worship for the throngs of investors from the retail sector who dumped their money into GME to fuel the upcoming short squeeze.

Contracts for calls allow you to purchase 100 shares specific stock at a set strike price. For example for example, a strike of 8 would be that Gill had the right to buy 100 shares GME with a price of $8 per contract bought. Also Gill earned profits from GME for as high over $8 it was. If Keith made a deposit of an amount of $53,000 to begin the position, it required him to purchase at the very most 1,000 call options at this $7 strike. Gill was able to control the gains from 100,000 shares of GME. As the price of GME climbed around $483. Gill's total profit is staggering.

Below, we've looked at the gains and losses of buying 100 shares, or eight strike calls. We've chosen a fairly random value for the cost of the eight strike calls which is $50. This is the maximum amount you can lose. In contrast it is possible to buy 100 shares for $880 per share, then you'd have to risk an additional $800 to gain the same upside.

It's crucial to be aware that call options carry more risky nature than shares and are encased in a variety of traps associated in their price The chart below helps to show that using only a tiny fraction of the funds necessary to buy shares Gill as well as other investors can achieve the same leverage. For the same price of $800 to purchase 100 shares, a person might be able to buy up to 16 calls. That's almost 16 times the amount of profit.

This will hopefully help to understand how certain individuals could have made insane amounts of money while they were up. This wasn't only through buying shares, but calls also were a major part of the tale.

As the Dr. Burry, Keith is a value-investor, meaning that he invests in companies that he believes are undervaluing because of an under-estimated risks. That, in turn will explain the origins of Keith's Reddit username. One of the videos posted on his channel, which was posted about five months prior to the events in January 2021, discusses the possibilities of a short squeeze taking the price up to $50 from $5... While this may be prophetic, it only reveals an eminent portion of what could happen. It was, however, an underestimate, and a bit of clairvoyance, the name was "The Big Short SQUEEZE from $5 to $50? Can GameStop share prices (GME) rise? It's a good investment"

The thing that makes Keith's acquisition of calls fascinating is the fact the fact that it plays into one of the major factors driving the GME rally, which is the"gamma squeeze. In a few sections we'll discuss this issue more in detail.

Keith has rationalized his actions in r/WSB, calling them an "YOLO." YOLO (You Only Live Once) plays are very popular in the subreddit he has called his home. It is believed that risk-averse traders will place bets on risky or high-reward plays on the assumption that they can earn a fortune even if they also lose everything which was sacrificed at the altar of sacrifice. This is the reason why they prefer choices, such as calls, as opposed to shares, they have significantly higher returns than shares.

While the two Burry and Keith were aboard the spacecraft, it was prepared for launch after another important investor bought a stake from mid-to-late 2020: Ryan Cohen.

Short Squeeze Short Squeeze With many institutions placing bets on the possibility of a hefty bid to lower the price, and some people who were convinced this was a good investment it was all established. The only thing required was a match to spark the fire of the short squeeze.

Before we get into the process and begin to teach the exact meaning of the short squeeze actually is. That's why we go into great detail about what shorts are but the second part won't be as difficult if you've already realized the concept. If you're not sure and need to go back through the chapter on short sales is helpful.

If lots of investors or businesses are short on an investment (like Melvin Capital, Citron, D1 Capital Partners, Mapleplan and Candlestick) If prices begin to climb to a significant extent, they have to purchase shares in order to pay for their short-term positions when the losses are too high for them to handle or simply aren't more complying with Regulation T due to failure to fulfill the requirements for margin 12. If they do not have sufficient capital to meet the growing minimal cash allocation the broker may be compelled to put them in margin calls and may even liquidate some their stock holdings in order to correct the issue.

When that happens it only gets more difficult for shorts of other types... because they are required to purchase shares they no longer wish to purchase, those who bet on a decline in the price of shares start to pressure the price of shares to go higher. The initial buying spurred by news of the bull market turns into buying driven by pressure from the short side.

In light of the fact that GameStop was short-interested at 121.9 percent as of the 15th day of January in addition to the fact that prominent investors such as Burry as well as Ryan Cohen had already disclosed their long positions, needed was an ounce of optimism for the stock to kick off an absolutely terrifying short squeeze13. There is no way to emphasize enough in the matter that the short interest was higher than 100%, meaning that investors purchasing shares from short sellers had the option of turning around to loan them for shorting yet.

Yes, short squeezes were common however, short interest that exceeds 100 percent is among the most dangerous and unnatural elements of the puzzle which the SEC is investigating to find out what regulatory actions could be taken to avoid the same thing from happening. It is a fact that the need for more shares was greater to pay for shorts than there were in circulation; once the shares were returned to the lender in some instances it was necessary for them to be returned to the person the lender acquired those shares from in initial transaction.

In the previous paragraph, Ryan Cohen, an early investor in the web-based pet products retailer, Chewy was a shareholder in GameStop early in the year 2020. purchasing 6.2 million shares or 9.6 percent of the company. By the time he was able to invest in Jan. 2021, he was more than just a shareholder as he received an advisory position on the board.

As Chewy has seen success due to its ability to market things online, it's no surprise that the web went viral over Ryan Cohen's active participation with the brick and mortar store. Ryan Cohen represented the hope that Chewy will become a new entity by becoming an online retailer of content and games as well as reduce costs in the process14.

Between the 12th and 14th of January between January 12th and 14th, the price of shares doubled due to the news and traded up to $19.95 to $39.91 and however, was only the start of the future.

The following few days, the price remained at the price level, holding about $40 per share. On reddit, the there was already enough recognition for u/DeepFuckingValue. His position proved to be correct -- and members of r/WSB also began to take his work more carefully.

On January 22 the shares were trading at $65. This was the point at which the story first circulated by Jim Cramer started to circulate like wildfire and it was Reddit users that caused the squeeze15 short.

This kind of trend began in the financial markets and the internet was aware of it was happening -- posts were coming in.

The 26th day of the month the shares were trading at $147.98 per share.

Perhaps the most shocking decision of the tale that day shares closed at $347.51 per piece. For a visual representation of these changes, go back to our page "Stock Charts" to see precisely what the squeeze was as for GameStop as well as a handful of other names that are relevant.

In the time period, Melvin Capital lost 53% of their value in the fund and sank to $8 billion of the assets they manage (AUM) from the initial $12.5 billion in AUM. The cushion to protect their halfing was the result out of the $2.75 Billion cash injection through Citadel and Point72. This means that without the injection their actual AUM may have dropped lower than the $6 billion mark.

It is still uncertain where this price rise actually originated from. Of course, some of the increase had to originate from Reddit customers who were thronging GameStop along with their assortment of other meme stocks which are now receiving media attention. The company became an holy fight: all together they wanted to prove with the guy, particularly in light of what was to happen on the 28th of January. However, there could or might not have been others who were big spenders behind the scenes, helping in pushing the stock prices upwards.

No matter who those investors who helped spread the short squeeze but there's a second important element of the picture that has to do with the huge volume of options of the businesses - the"gamma squeeze.

Chapter 7: Gamma Squeeze

Short sales may be a problem for companies such as Melvin Capital, gamma squeezes could cause a complete disaster. Without this element the shares would not have risen close to the peak of $483.

Stock options, similar to those calls u/DeepFuckingValue wanted has a price that is determined according to"the "Greeks." These are the models that determine the cost of calls depending on the changes of various elements, including the value of stock. Two of the most important Greeks include gamma and delta.

Delta is the factor that determines the cost of the option, dependent on the rise in the price of stock. If the delta is +.04 indicates that the option's value will go up by $4.00 per dollar gain in the price of the stock. To calculate the delta is to divide .04

by 100. That's how many shares which the call option has leverage over.

Although a 4 percent increase for each dollar of increase in stock might not be too crazy the delta isn't very high. Options on call that are purchased using strikes close to the price of the stock are deltas that range from +.50. It means that for every increment in price it will increase the cost of the call by 50 dollars per contract. Additionally, a high "In The Money" (ITM) call has more of a delta than 1.00. That's $100 increment in the value of the call for every dollar of increase in the value of the stock.

Like you could sell a stock short as well, you could also short an option call. Thus, major institutions offer large quantities of call options, with low deltas to the retail investor in anticipation that they will expire worthless. It's usually lucrative: offering useless options for investors who do not know the nuances of what they're selling. But there's a second element to this puzzle... Gamma.

Gamma is the factor that determines a delta's value from to +.04 to up to +1.00. If delta value is +.04 and gamma +.01 and for each increment in dollars of the stock it is not just that the stock go up $4.00 however, the delta also rises by +.01.

For the following increment in dollars, the contract will increase to $5.00 in value instead of $4.00. After that, the next dollar will have the contract increase by $6.00 each time a dollar is increased.

It may seem slow, although gamma does increase. If delta is +.50 the gamma ranges between +.02 or +.03 However, this could differ greatly. There's generally a significant increase in gamma you're looking at options that close to the expiration date.

Even though delta is a finite number, and never exceeds +1.00 however, it is able to be able to go from +.01 all the way to this figure in a short time if the stock increases up to $50 per day. Naturally, this could be used by the smart investor who is able to accidentally push the price higher.

In the past, companies have to sell calls in order so that investors can purchase the calls. If a company sells calls, they will protect it by purchasing shares in line with the delta of their loss to make up for it. As an example, if GME is at $30 per share, and a buyer purchases the call at 50 strike and a delta +.04 and the company that sells the call would purchase four shares. This way, for each one cent increase in the price it will compensate for their loss from the growth in value of the call by an increase in share price.

A purchase of four shares isn't going to change the price of the most under-traded security. However, if there are thousands of investors buying call in order to get their rich scheme, it is possible that the price increase by a tiny amount as banks take a risk by securing the price. With short-term rate of interest that is over 100%, even a tiny amount can be enough.

The weakest of shorts starts to give way due to the combination of retail's desire and the buying of shares by institutions portion, perhaps the price will rise to $31 for each share.

Now, the delta of those strike calls of 50 becomes +.05. The institutions who sold the calls usually keep computers on standby to purchase just one additional shares of the company of interest. Be aware that the call was sold is now increasing 5 cents for each dollar that the stock gains and they now have to buy 5 shares instead of 4 shares to keep up with the increase in the worth of their short-term positions.

With many thousands of outstanding short calls that could result in automatic share purchases that are in the six figures for each dollar increment in the stock that is underlying.

A computer is a gamma squeeze. It covers an organization's risk by investing in the stock's going downwards, however it will not end up going higher17. Therefore, it's not just investors that are often forced to buy back shares in exchange for each short share and there are businesses that have short-calls that may need to purchase several shares per increment in price of a dollar.

More and more businesses are supplying the flame. So, the artillery assault from a squeeze becomes into a nuclear blast when a gamma-squeeze is also beginning to occur. Because gamma squeezes are typically automated, it is common to find trading algorithms purchasing at whatever price the market is. The modern trading software because of its binary and static nature, may not perform as it should in an ever-changing market. For short sellers, this could be the most difficult thing to do. They're now not just taking cover while the other short sellers cover as well, but they're also fighting machines that are chasing shares. This means that the chances of margin calls as well as emotional investment have increased. Both of them are the biggest enemies of the money manager of any size.

There was no doubt that a handful of users of r/WSB were aware of this, and shared information to other investors through messages. The goal was to get the stock over key strike prices that witnessed a large number of calls that were short, the most specifically $115 and $220 because they believed that this would result in more pressures on gamma and cause the stock surge higher.

For clarity The gamma squeeze may be stopped. The issue would be for many businesses but, they would have to recover the loss on call options they sold.

Keep this all in the back of our minds, this kind of artificial price inflation may be as dramatic in its path to a lower level, as witnessed during the first week of February. If the gamma and delta would drop dramatically on the short-term options that firms offered Many algorithms will immediately sell any excess GME shares that these companies needed to purchase, exactly as they would have purchased them. The 29th of January on Friday the estimated number of 13.3 million shares (of the 69.75 million floating) were in the hands of firms that were part of a hedge strategy.

Pushback -- Freezing Trades

In the wake of the combined storm of the gamma and short squeezes, on Wednesday the 27th of January There were requests for shares in singles at GameStop that were being fulfilled at up to $5200 per share. That is to say, the buying pressure was nearly endless.

And then, things changed. Over the course of the week, big box brokers including Charles Scwhab and TD Ameritrade have been placing restrictions on the kinds and amounts of trades they allow on their platforms with respect to GameStop. But, Robinhood, the broker that was previously praised by a lot members of Wall Street Bets users who applied pressure to this short squeeze had to stop the opening of trades with GameStop, AMC, Nokia and the other stocks that were being squeezed by traders who were retail on the day on Thursday, January 28,18. The only thing that retail traders could do was to close out their positions.

The seemingly innocuous decision has triggered immediately controversy, and backlash by anyone who has a Twitter account. In an unusual moment of political harmony within a divided country Alexandria Ocasio Cortez (AOC) was one of the Democratic Congresswoman of New York, was retweeted by Ted Cruz, a Republican Senator from Texas.

One of the initial issues that came up in the minds of many during the Thursday debate was Robinhood's history of selling its order flows to Citadel and not revealing that they were doing it. It is a sign that a significant portion of its trades were sold to Citadel that runs a huge group of hedge funds. as a result, Robinhood provided

Citadel with crucial information that it to earn a profit from.

For instance in this case, in the event that Citadel was aware that 300,000 shares of the company were going to be sold by retailers They could purchase it and earn on the increase in price once they have finished the transaction. This is referred to in the industry as "front running" and is prohibited.

In the month of July, 2020 Citadel was required to settle a fine of $700,000 in connection with this particular infraction 19. It is debatable whether or not this amount will be enough to deter the business from continuing to practice it is debateable. However, at the at the same time, it's probable that, if the SEC had come back another time, the sanction will be much far more serious than a simple handshake and a danger it is impossible to imagine that Citadel could be ignorant of.

In the end, for Robinhood If the app transfer its orders to market-makers such as Citadel the company is legally liable for the disclosure of the transfer to their clients. In the month of December, 2020 the SEC issued the company with an amount of $65 million due to the failure to share the fact to customers in the years 2015-201820. Even though Robinhood continues to sell the flow in this manner but now they're publicizing it, it's legally to be legal.

One of the criticisms against this method is that, since Robinhood earns a profit per trade however small the amount, they're encouraged to increase the amount of transactions made with every account, to maximize the profit they make.

In their capacity as a Broker-Dealer registered with the CFTC It is their obligation to comply with an "suitability requirement" to make sure that trades executed fit their clients since customers who make trading are expected to be customers of the broker rather than the market makers to whom they are selling orders flow to. This is why there have been allegations that this is an act of conflict of interest. If a broker attempts to earn money through selling large quantities of trades in order to make money for the market maker, they will be encouraged to promote trades regardless of whether they are suitable or ineffective the trades may be to their clients.

One of the factors that began to create confusion in the debate over why trading stopped was Citadel's bailout for Melvin Capital. We've already discussed that Melvin Capital had one of the largest short positions in GameStop. On the 25th of January, that GameStop was trading at $76 per share Citadel offered Melvin with another $2 billion of liquidity together with a further $750 million that was received from the company Steve Cohen, a hedge fund manager, and a former coach of Gabe Plotkin, Melvin's manager.

In light of the fact that Robinhood has strong connections to Citadel and Citadel was now a major player in having GameStop restore to a regular price so it's not a surprise that the internet began to flutter with accusations of the involvement of foul action. Elon Musk and Chamath Palihapitya Donald Trump Junior, and Ja Rule took to Twitter to speak about the situation.

It was discovered this evening on Thursday that the increase in new customers created a liquidity problem at their side also. To allow instant trading to users the default of Robinhood is to create accounts that have margin capabilities, which require that the broker hold collateral, which is essentially money, per account.

Due to the flood of accounts being opened, Robinhood couldn't maintain the clearing house's requirements. To address this issue it was necessary for the company seek a billion dollar capital infusion to enable customers to trade 21.

Although this does not seem to eliminate the possibility of collusion Citadel but Twitter's fury over the matter was not able to stop. There was at least one suit initiated against Robinhood on the very same Thursday as well as an investigation by Congress to a few brokers over the option to restrict trading on the stocks mentioned above.

Chapter 8: A Take on the Events

The following article will explain what transpired in the Big Short Squeeze, but what do these events suggest? In the wake of this Congressional Testimony that included Ken Griffin, Keith Gill, Vlad Tenev, Gabriel Plotkin as well as a host of other players who were involved on February 18, 2014 and the implications of the events are still at the moment.

A concern raised from Rep. David Scott of Georgia is the fact that markets are now extremely susceptible to inaccurate information being spread on the web The spread of a false rumor may alter the value of crypto currencies and stocks over a shorter period of time more than any research could do.

Although this certainly is an issue, we've decided to concentrate on two additional areas highlighted through the incidents: poor handling of tail risk, and the promotion of trading not supported with due diligence.

Hedging Against Seen and Unseen Risk

The stock market is a risky place There aren't any guarantees of return; there's none of the certainty, and it is impossible to ensure everything. As an investor that it is your obligation to keep moving by focusing on this one truth and scrutinizing and rethinking every decisions you make. No day can be passed without being asked "And what happens if I'm wrong?"

This view of market risk was greatly influenced Nassim Nicholas Taleb's book, The Black Swan: The Implications of the The Almost Improbable. The book discusses The truth about the subject is that there isn't all the facts required to make predictions about the future. Investors and traders both institutional and retail alike always fall short. Although you are able to make predictions regarding the future, as long as those assumptions are tempering by the most extreme level of suspicion and shielded against uncertainty using carefully planned bets that are based on the facts which you anticipate to occur and you, as an investor can be at risk more than you are willing to acknowledge.

www.ingramcontent.com/pod-product-compliance
Lightning Source LLC
Chambersburg PA
CBHW071220210326
41597CB00016B/1885